PURITY RISES FROM ABOVE

THE SIMPLE TRUTH TO OBTAIN FREEDOM FROM BONDAGE TO SIN AND RESTORE PURITY TO SEXUALITY

Yeshua S. Jehu

Yeshua S. Jehu

Appreciation

To God Almighty, who in His infinite grace has granted me divine revelations, timely resources, strengthening counsel, and unwavering guidance through every season. I give profound thanks for His abundant wisdom, faithfulness, and sovereign hand that has sustained, inspired, and carried this work from inception to completion. All glory belongs to Him alone.

Contents

VISION FOR THE BOOK

Human society is built upon three foundational pillars upon which influence and power draw their source in this world. Those pillars are **Finance, Sexuality, and Religion**. For the church to walk in power, exert godly influence, carry out holy change in the earth, and protect God's sacred interests, it must hold a firm grip at the helm of these three pillars—establishing them in righteousness.

This has been the mandate of God from the very beginning when He fashioned mankind and entrusted the earth to them: *"Then God blessed them, and God said to them, 'Be fruitful and multiply; fill the earth and subdue it; have dominion over the fish of the sea, over the birds of the air, and over every living thing that moves on the earth.'"* (Genesis 1:28, NKJV)

By "be fruitful," we see the faith-based pillar. "Be fruitful" extends beyond reproduction and prosperity; it reaches into the spiritual fabric of a life that bears fruit in character and deed—love, kindness, righteousness, service, and every holy outworking of the Spirit. It speaks of the fruits of the Holy Spirit *(Galatians 5:22–23)* and the true "religion" that God accepts, expressed through purity, compassion, and obedience *(James 1:27)*. This is the pillar of faith, devotion, and spiritual alignment.

Another pillar embedded in this mandate is **Finance**: "subdue" the earth. Humanity cannot subdue the earth without wealth, for wealth grants access to resources, tools, and infrastructures that enable dominion in the physical world. Scripture affirms this divine arrangement:

"And you shall remember the LORD your God, for it is He who gives you power to get wealth, that He may establish His covenant which He swore to your fathers, as it is this day." (Deuteronomy 8:18, NKJV) This covenant traces back to Abraham, to whom God promised dominion—dominion over nations and influence in the earth *(Genesis 22:17)*. Wealth becomes the instrument through which that covenantal dominion is carried forward in our physical realm.

But the pillar that stands as the focal point of this book is **Sexuality**: "Multiply; fill the earth." Notice the divine progression—**be fruitful**, then **multiply**, then **subdue**, and as the culmination: **have dominion**. Whoever influences these pillars wields dominion in the earth.

This is why the kingdom of darkness tirelessly labors to infiltrate and occupy the seats of global wealth, propagate false religion, and—especially in our generation—wage relentless war over sexuality. Sexuality remains one of the most contested territories because it is the pillar from which all humanity emerges and from which natural identity is shaped. Whoever holds influence over sexuality possesses significant influence over the very formation and direction of human society.

Thus, the vision of this book is clear: **to shed the light of purity upon sexuality**, to edify, equip, and set free the believer from the cords of darkness that seek to corrupt and rule this God-ordained pillar. It is a clarion call for the Church of Christ to rise, reclaim, and re-establish righteous influence over sexuality as a central pillar of human society. Only then can purity rise from above and bring healing, order, and dominion back into the hands of the righteous.

PREFACE

Sexuality

Sexuality is the springboard upon which all humanity draws its natural source and natural identity. It is God's created design that distinguishes us—male from female—granting us definition and forming the foundation upon which God built all human society, giving us the opportunity to work together, multiply, fill the earth, and therefore wield influence through its power.

Within sexuality lies God's sacred gift to humanity: marriage, which encompasses both biological and spiritual dimensions. It refers primarily to the procreative and unitive relationship between one man and one woman within the covenant of marriage. Sexuality, as ordained by God, is meant to express intimacy, mutual love, and covenantal bonding—reflecting the holy union He established from the beginning:

"So God created man in His own image; in the image of God He created him; male and female He created them" and *"Be fruitful and multiply; fill the earth and subdue it"* (Genesis 1:27–28, NKJV), together with the divine joining of husband and wife into "one flesh" *(Genesis 2:24; Matthew 19:4–6).*

By God's own design as the Creator of sex, sexual expression is only appropriate within the permanent, faithful, monogamous marriage between a man and a woman. Sexual union serves both for the purpose of procreation and for strengthening the marital bond.

Yet it also points to a deeper spiritual mystery: the marital relationship reflects Christ's love for the Church *(Ephesians 5:22–33)*. Even the climax of intimacy between a husband and wife serves as an explanatory typification—a God-crafted metaphor—to help humanity grasp the depth, surrender, and sacred ecstasy found in true worship between man and God.

God's Word—the Creator's manual for holy human living—upholds that humanity is made male and female, a binary gender design intended by God. Sexuality expresses this divine distinction in both physical and relational dimensions. It is not merely physical, but emotional and spiritual, crafted to bring unity that is pure, life-giving, and in full honor of God's intent for His creation.

Christian sexuality, therefore, is the God-ordained expression of love, intimacy, and procreation within the covenant of marriage—marked by faithfulness and reflecting God's creative and redemptive purposes for human relationships.

Purpose of the Book

The purpose of this book is to bring much-needed counsel on sexual purity in a world steeped in sexual perversion—not only to keep believers anchored in the purity of Christ and away from sexual sin, but also to equip them with the practical and spiritual tools necessary to guard their purity both before and during marriage. Through revelation from the Word of

God and practical wisdom grounded in Scripture, this book empowers believers to stand against sexual corruption and prevail in the power of purity.

There are simple yet often hidden truths about the ease and clarity of attaining and maintaining sexual purity. This book will unveil those truths and guarantees—should you take initiative with firm resolve—that *"the truth shall set you free" (John 8:32).* It will guide you in how to maintain sexual purity in life and in preparation for, and in, marriage, how to overcome lust, and how to attain wholesome sexual wellness within the purity of Christ.

The goal is to keep the chaff of sexual impurity—born from the world's corrupted handling of sexuality—from harming, weakening, and ultimately destroying your life and your future marriage, by addressing these matters long before destruction can take root.

Tragically, as the Church has shrunk back from speaking boldly on the topic of sex, the world has raised its voice even louder—yet in the most corrupted and perverse sense. This has led to the distortion of sexuality and the collapse of structures that once upheld righteous and pure living. God has entrusted the stewardship of purity and sexual teaching to His people.

The Church is the ordained institution responsible for faithfully teaching sexuality according to God's design. When it fails to uphold these teachings—teachings that influence one of the most vital pillars of human society—multitudes are lost to sexual sin, and corruption festers even deeper into the fabric of the world.

The Church must rise and reclaim its rightful place at the helm of influence over these defining pillars that determine the moral health of society, redirecting them back to the path of righteousness. The Church must counter the world's loudness regarding sexuality by refusing to shrink back. Every generation perishes when the Church sits on the sidelines.

Our children are discipled by the world, and the Church itself becomes polluted when lies about sexuality seep into its walls, subtly corroding the structures of righteousness and reshaping them into forms more palatable to worldly preferences. If proclaiming the truth makes one unpopular, then so be it—for only the truth of God can set the souls of humankind free.

CHRIST'S LOYAL VASSAL,

JEHU :')

INTRODUCTION
PURITY RISES FROM ABOVE

Our quest for purity and our fight against the desires of the flesh are futile unless we acknowledge our weakness and run to depend fully on growing into the fullness of Christ within us—a transformation that can only be achieved by relying entirely on the Holy Spirit. The Holy Spirit was sent to remind us, to testify of Christ, and—remarkably—He does not speak of His own accord but only what He hears the Father say. *(John 16:13)*

Now, the Father speaks His Word, and if the Spirit only speaks what He hears from the Father, then He only speaks the Word of God to you. How, then, will you relate to His person—One whose entire communication is rooted in the precepts of God's Word in your life—if you do not have the Word of God within you?

How else will you grow into the fullness of the stature of Christ and ascend into that higher plane of spiritual stance where true purity is found, if the Word of God is not established in you as a lifestyle discipline that is continually renewed?

How else will you grow? Having learned this, you cannot count your safety based on the measures you take to secure your sexual purity and integrity, for no matter how drastic those measures are, the sinful nature will always attempt to find you—even if it is years later. What then is the solution?

The solution, as we will see, is *spiritual growth*—where you attain God-given strength to resist the sinful nature and eventually, by the power of the Holy Spirit living within you, put it to death so that the life of Christ may abound in you. Only then can you live above the base principles of this world, lest you crumble back into the old sinful patterns and rekindle the very nature the Spirit came to crucify.

We are therefore called to total dependence on the Holy Spirit, and to do this, a life rooted in the Word of God is indispensable. The Word is the foundational resource the Holy Spirit uses after salvation to grow you. The Word of God is the food of your newborn spirit, and the Spirit Himself acts as the Producer of the divine 'growth hormones' that enable spiritual maturity as you feed your inner man.

The purpose of fervent reading is so that your mind remains fruitful and constantly remembers the Word of God, enabling you to consciously walk in His precepts in every aspect of life. A *precept* is a general rule that regulates behavior or thought. Through fervent reading of Scripture—as I will continually exhort you through this book—your mind remains vigilant, sensitive to the leading of the Holy Spirit, and anchored to the path of purity.

The reason for repeated and consistent reading disciplines is that you, as a child of the Most High God—a king and a priest unto the Almighty—might not stumble into sin, but continually renew your mind with God's righteous precepts.

"When he takes the throne of his kingdom, he is to write for himself on a scroll a copy of this law... It is to be with him, and he is to read it all the days of his life..." (Deuteronomy 17:18–19, NIV) This continual reading would keep the king from pride, from drifting into sin, and ensure generational stability. And as it was commanded for him, so it is commanded for you. You must read—rinse and repeat—so as not to falter.

We are called to lean not on our own understanding but to acknowledge Him in all our ways. *"Trust in the LORD with all your heart and lean not on your own understanding; in all your ways submit to Him, and He will make your paths straight."* (Proverbs 3:5–6, NIV)

There is no rock strong enough, no refuge secure enough, except Christ Jesus, the Hope of Glory. When it comes to sexual integrity and purity, it is not how much we do to protect ourselves; *true purity must rise from above*—from walking by the Spirit so that we do not gratify the desires of the flesh, and by clothing ourselves in Christ through the cleansing waters of the Word. This speaks not only of sexual purity but purity in all your affairs.

"So I say, walk by the Spirit, and you will not gratify the desires of the flesh. For the flesh desires what is contrary to the Spirit, and the Spirit what is contrary to the flesh. They are in conflict with each other, so that you are not to do whatever you want. But if you are led by the Spirit, you are not under the law." (Galatians 5:16–18, NIV)

It is only when you grow deeper in Christlikeness that you ascend into that higher plane of spiritual stature where you are clothed with Christ Himself. This clothing occurs when the mind is continually renewed and matured by the cleansing water of the Word. *"...clothe yourselves with the Lord Jesus Christ, and do not think about how to gratify the desires of the flesh." (Romans 13:14, NIV)*

Christ is, according to *John 1*, the *Word made flesh.* You cannot clothe yourself with Him—thus gaining the ability to refuse the thoughts that gratify the sinful nature—without reading and internalizing the Word of God. Every prudent believer who desires victory over the flesh and a life of uncompromised purity must cultivate disciplined reading of Scripture and spiritual maturity through prayer.

"We demolish arguments and every pretension that sets itself up against the knowledge of God, and we take captive every thought to make it obedient to Christ." (2 Corinthians 10:5, NIV)

As you journey through life, you will eventually enter the marital season. It is paramount that you walk by the Spirit, for the enemy is aware of this sacred season and seeks fiercely to corrupt it. He will attempt to introduce counterfeits. Only a life matured in the Word can elevate you above the reach of impurity.

Whether married, preparing for marriage, or single, sexual purity is essential because the unhealthier your purity is, the unhealthier your life and marriage will be. *Unhealthy people create unhealthy marriages.* Therefore, cleansing your stance on sexuality with the Word of God is non-negotiable.

When you lean on anything other than Christ the Rock, sexual sin will follow. It will devour the fruits of your hard-earned achievements in God or otherwise, for sin is the virus of Satan—the one who comes only *"to steal, kill, and destroy" (John 10:10)*—and this is exactly what impurity will seek to do. It brings shame and humiliation because of neglecting the Spirit's voice and feeding the weakness of the flesh. Only *purity that rises from above* can keep the fruit-eating nature of sin far from you.

Your purity can only be truly effective when you give yourself entirely to the Holy Spirit, and as we have established, this can only be done through the power of the Word—fueling the spiritual growth required to rise into a higher plane of stamina where the lusts of the flesh are subdued beneath your spirit. Then you will stand upon the precepts of God and declare with authority that:

'Purity Rises from Above!'

CHAPTER 1
THE WORD OF GOD FOR SPIRITUAL GROWTH

It is a principle that for anything to grow, it must be fed. The same is true for your inner man—your spirit—who is born after you receive the gift of salvation. It is a new identity, a person; it is who you are in Christ. Yet this new life must be fed in order to grow, so that it can sustain the life of purity and righteousness required to walk the journey of salvation and to do the holy work of God for which you have been redeemed.

There exists, however, an enemy to your spirit-man. This enemy is called the sinful nature. Though your spirit desires to do the things that please Christ because you have been redeemed, the spirit-man is constantly opposed and often overcome by the vicious strength of the sinful nature.

It overpowers you so that you end up doing the wrong things and desiring them over what is true, pure, and righteous. The sinful nature is the embodiment of sin in your life. It came as the result of the fall of man from the garden of Eden and exists solely to rebel against God. It serves as the key platform, facilitator, and abode of evil and demonic footholds in your life.

When it comes to sexual integrity—sexual purity—it is not about how much we do to protect ourselves from the sinful nature's prevalence. Our true purity can only rise from above. "Above" being the vantage point of walking by the Spirit so that we may not gratify the desires of the sinful nature, and clothing ourselves with Christlikeness. This then ushers you into a higher plane of spiritual stature and strength to maintain purity. It speaks of more than sexual purity alone, but purity in all your affairs.

Thus, only a spirit-man developed and matured through feeding on the Word of God will have the strength to overcome the sinful nature. For as the Word of God is growth-food for your spirit, it is also a killing toxin to the sinful nature—because that which is righteous will always purge its environment of darkness.

The Word of God for Purity

Purity is a divine gift bestowed by God, yet it is not a passive state but an altar demanding continuous sacrifice and cleansing. Christ Himself is the eternal gift sustaining this altar—your intimate relationship with Him. It is within this sacred union that you plant the seed of God's Word, allowing it to bear fruit and consistently renew your purity. The washing of the water of the Word upon your mind cultivates purity of thought, as Philippians 4:8 (NKJV) urges us:

"Finally, brethren, whatever things are true, whatever things are noble, whatever things are just, whatever things are pure, whatever things are lovely, whatever things are of good report, if there is any virtue and if there is anything praiseworthy—meditate on these things." Such purity clears the mind

of impurities introduced by sinful thoughts, granting a spiritual vision untainted by worldly distortion. Purity begins in the mind—by focusing on what is true, honest, and pure. The pure heart and mind align with God's standards, enabling us to see rightly and resist spiritual deception.

When the Word of God dwells richly within us, it acts as a shield—a divine filter—guarding us from impurities that seep in through sinful thoughts and worldly influences, thus keeping the spiritual vision clear and undistorted. As 2 Peter 3:1–2 (NKJV) reminds us, *"Beloved, I now write to you this second epistle (in both of which I stir up your pure minds by way of reminder), that you may be mindful of the words which were spoken before by the holy prophets, and of the commandment of us, the apostles of the Lord and Savior."*

The apostles wrote to stir up our pure minds by way of remembrance, encouraging us to be mindful of God's holy words spoken through the prophets and apostles. The Spirit of God alone understands the depths of His thoughts, as 1 Corinthians 2:11 (NIV) declares: *"For who knows a person's thoughts except their own spirit within them? In the same way no one knows the thoughts of God except the Spirit of God."* He alone guides our understanding as we grow in knowledge.

Our instruction is aimed at love growing out of a pure heart, a good conscience, and sincere faith, as 1 Timothy 1:5 (NIV) affirms: *"The goal of this command is love, which comes from a pure heart and a good conscience and a sincere faith."* This shows that purity is not merely external but springs from a transformed inner being.

How then do we maintain a pure mind? Psalm 119:9 provides the crucial answer: *"How can a young person stay pure? By obeying your word."* (NLT) The Word of God is the cleansing agent—a spiritual water that washes away impurity when we diligently apply it to our lives. Isaiah 26:3 (NKJV) promises, *"You will keep him in perfect peace, whose mind is stayed on You, because he trusts in You."*

The psalmist beautifully prays in Psalm 139:23–24 (NKJV), *"Search me, O God, and know my heart; Try me, and know my anxieties; And see if there is any wicked way in me, and lead me in the way everlasting."* In this, he asks God to search, know, and lead him away from wickedness onto the everlasting path.

Desires of the flesh and temptations act as heavy weights that hinder, seeking to drag us down and extinguish spiritual fervor. We, as believers, face this relentless battle because we are called to live contrary to the governing principles of this world. Yet many lose this battle simply because we lack the knowledge and revelation of the Word of God to withstand.

Christ's example in the wilderness reveals the pathway to victory: reliance on the Holy Spirit and unyielding adherence to Scripture. Matthew 4:1–11 (NKJV) vividly demonstrates this:

"Then Jesus was led up by the Spirit into the wilderness to be tempted by the devil. And when He had fasted forty days and forty nights, afterward He was hungry. Now when the tempter came to Him, he said, 'If You are the Son of God, command that these stones become bread.' But He answered and said, 'It is written, "Man shall not live by bread alone, but by every word that proceeds from the mouth of God."' Then the devil took Him up into the holy city, set Him on the pinnacle of the temple, and said to Him, 'If You are the Son of God, throw Yourself down. For it is written: "He shall give His angels charge over you," and, "In their hands they shall bear you up, lest you dash your foot against a stone."' Jesus said to him, 'It is written again, "You shall not tempt the LORD your God."' Again, the devil took Him up

on an exceedingly high mountain, and showed Him all the kingdoms of the world and their glory. And he said to Him, 'All these things I will give You if You will fall down and worship me.' Then Jesus said to him, 'Away with you, Satan! For it is written, "You shall worship the LORD your God, and Him only you shall serve."' Then the devil left Him, and behold, angels came and ministered to Him."

Christ did not engage Satan in debate; He defeated temptation through the power of God's Word. This instructs us that conquering lust and impurity is not a matter of willpower but of surrender to God's truth.

Through this foundation of Scripture, the washing of the Word will cleanse and fortify your mind for spiritual strength in purity. As we prepare to dive deeper into Psalm 119—the inspired Word extolling the power of God's law to produce holiness and strength—may you be encouraged that the path to purity is secured by abiding in the Word of God.

THE WORD THAT MATURES: SPIRITUAL STRENGTH FOR A PURE MIND

Psalm 119 (NLT)

Psalm 119 is a profound declaration of the power of God's Word to nurture spiritual purity and strength. The opening verses establish the foundation for this truth. Verse 2 says, *"Joyful are those who obey his laws and search for him with all their hearts,"* revealing that a wholehearted pursuit of God, marked by obedience to His commands, brings genuine joy. This joy is not superficial but grows from a deep, intimate relationship with God, cultivated through reverence for His Word.

Verse 3 continues, *"They do not compromise with evil and they walk only in his paths,"* showing that purity means steadfastness—walking unwaveringly in God's ways without compromise. The psalmist frames obedience as a safeguard that keeps us from the entanglements of sin.

Verse 9 then asks the piercing question, *"How can a young person stay pure? By obeying your word,"* shining a direct spotlight on the Word of God as the means to maintain purity. It is not knowledge alone but obedience to His Word that preserves us. Verse 11 confirms this: *"I have hidden your word in my heart that I might not sin against you,"* portraying the internalization of Scripture as the barrier against sin.

This section establishes a critical principle: those who keep God's law in their hearts and obey every word build a spiritual fortress around their being. Feeding on the Word brings protection and maturity. Verse 26 echoes a heartfelt prayer: *"I told you my plans and you answered; now teach me your decrees,"* acknowledging that guidance comes through knowing God's statutes, not human wisdom.

Verse 29 pleads, *"Keep me from lying to myself; give me the privilege of knowing your instructions,"* highlighting self-deception as a key spiritual danger and emphasizing the necessity of divine revelation for true understanding. Verse 32 declares, *"I will pursue your commands for you expand my understanding,"* affirming that pursuing God's commands leads to growing insight.

The psalmist warns against relying on one's own understanding, echoing Hosea 4:6 (NKJV) where God laments, *"My people are destroyed for lack of knowledge."* With God's Word, we gain the knowledge needed to resist sin and not perish under the weight of fleshly lusts.

Verse 36 presents a transformation of desires: *"Give me an eagerness for your laws rather than a love for money,"* while verse 37 adds, *"Turn my eyes from worthless things and give me life through your word."* The Word redirects our affections from materialism and empty pursuits to vibrant spiritual life, equipping us to overcome even subtle temptations such as the love of money. This teaches that purity extends beyond sexuality—it touches every dimension of life, including financial integrity.

Verses 39 and 40 offer a plea for renewal: *"Help me abandon my shameful ways, for your regulations are good,"* and *"I long to obey your commands; renew my life with your goodness."* The goodness of God's law invites repentance, cleansing, and restoration. Verse 45 proclaims the blessing of freedom: *"I will walk in freedom, for I have devoted myself to your commandments,"* teaching us that obedience to Scripture leads to true liberty—not bondage.

Verse 59 recounts reflection and decision: *"I pondered the direction of my life and I turned to follow your laws,"* while verse 75 recognizes divine discipline: *"I know, O LORD, that your regulations are fair; you disciplined me because I needed it."* These passages reveal that the Word of God is not only a guide but also a source of correction, shaping our lives into alignment with righteousness.

As Paul reminds Timothy in *2 Timothy 3:16–17 (NLT): "All Scripture is inspired by God and is useful to teach us what is true and to make us realize what is wrong in our lives. It corrects us when we are wrong and teaches us to do what is right. God uses it to prepare and equip his people to do every good work."* The Word disciplines, directs, cleanses, and empowers for purity.

Verse 89 affirms the enduring nature of God's Word: *"Your eternal Word, O Lord, stands firm in heaven."* Verse 104 marvels, *"Your commandments give me understanding; no wonder I hate every false way of life,"* while verse 105 assures, *"Your word is a lamp to guide my feet and a light for my path."*

These truths resonate with Paul's testimony in Galatians 6:14 (NLT): *"As for me, may I never boast about anything except the cross of our Lord Jesus Christ. Because of that cross, my interest in this world has been crucified, and the world's interest in me has also died."*

The Word illumines the path of righteousness and calls us to the ancient ways of holiness, as *Jeremiah 6:16 (NIV)* commands: *"Stand at the crossroads and look; ask for the ancient paths, ask where the good way is, and walk in it, and you will find rest for your souls. But you said, 'We will not walk in it.'"* Rejecting God's Word is rejecting the way; embracing it grants vision and direction.

Verses 130, 133, and 165 affirm God's Word as the source of enlightenment and protection: *"The teaching of your words gives light; so even the simple can understand."* (verse 130). *"Guide my steps by your word, so I will not be overcome by evil"* (verse 133). *"Those who love your instructions have great peace and do not stumble."* (verse 165).

Therefore, walking in the Word is walking in purity—shielded by the holiness of the Most High. It is a vibrant, living power that cleanses and sustains the redeemed spirit. This grace in Christ alone is the foundation of true sexual and spiritual purity.

THE SINFUL NATURE DEMYSTIFIED

The sinful nature is a product of the rebellion and fall of man from the Garden of Eden. It is an entity of the fallen world and a nature embedded in each and every one of us. It is therefore also referred to as the Adamic nature, named after the first man Adam who disobeyed God and was cast out of the Garden of Eden along with his wife Eve. It is the abode of evil in our lives and is the makeup of the image of what our lives appeared like to God before we received salvation.

The sinful nature is not to be confused with the physical body. It is important to mark the difference. The physical flesh has nothing wrong with it; it is merely a body occupied and controlled by your spirit. It therefore cannot sin, but we sin against it through sexual sin. The "lust" of the "flesh" spoken of in the Bible is not referring to the physical flesh, but to the sinful nature. The Greek makes this easier by classifying the two. The physical body is called *(Soma)*, and the sinful nature is called *(Sarx)*.

The *(Soma)* is but a body we leave behind when we die; it then becomes lifeless and cannot sin. Who then does the sin? It is the sinful nature,*(Sarx)*. For we know that there is a war between the *(Sarx)* and the spirit-man born of the Holy Spirit through faith in Christ Jesus: *"For the flesh desires what is contrary to the Spirit, and the Spirit what is contrary to the flesh. They are in conflict with each other, so that you are not to do whatever you want."* (Galatians 5:17 NIV).

See, it is a tug of war for your life—one pulling towards sin, the other towards purity. Your physical body plays no part, but heed the side that overcomes. If your spirit is not mature in holding fast to the Spirit of God's leading, then you will be pulled into the *(Sarx's)* lusts, and you will be made subject to the law of sin and death: *"But if you are led by the Spirit, you are not under the law."* (Galatians 5:18 NIV).

In Romans 7:14-17, the apostle Paul speaks of this same struggle and sheds light on this truth. The sinful nature is sin living within you: *"We know that the law is spiritual; but I am unspiritual, sold as a slave to sin. I do not understand what I do. For what I want to do I do not do, but what I hate I do. And if I do what I do not want to do, I agree that the law is good. As it is, it is no longer I myself who do it, but it is sin living in me."* (Romans 7:14-17 NIV).

The work of the sinful nature is to keep you in bondage to sin because this is where its lifeblood and sustenance are located. It does not want you to walk the path of righteousness, for that would be the death of it. Being part of your fallen human nature, it will seek to self-protect by luring you into its safe space—"sin." Do not condescend to it. Mature in strength to overcome its strength.

Paul teaches in Romans 6:16 that we become slaves to the side we succumb to: *"Don't you know that when you offer yourselves to someone as obedient slaves, you are slaves of the one you obey—whether you are slaves to sin, which leads to death, or to obedience, which leads to righteousness?"* (Romans 6:16 NIV).

It is for this reason we are exhorted in Romans 6:10-14 to live above it, not letting it reign anymore. This is rising above—attaining the higher plane of spiritual stature where true and sustainable purity rises in your life from:

"The death He died, he died to sin once for all; but the life He lives, He lives to God. In the same way, count yourselves dead to sin but alive to God in Christ Jesus. Therefore do not let sin reign in your mortal body so that you

obey its evil desires. Do not offer any part of yourself to sin, as an instrument of wickedness, but rather offer yourselves to God, as those who have been brought from death to life; and offer every part of yourself to Him as an instrument of righteousness. For sin shall no longer be your master, because you are not under the law, but under grace." (Romans 6:10-14 NIV).

Therefore, if you truly desire to live a life free of bondage to sin—a life of sustainable purity, not temporary seasons of seriousness that end in discouragement—you must rise to the place of spiritual strength by maturing in the Word of God. This is also the place where one can finally crucify the sinful nature.

The sinful nature can only lead you away from God because it can only lead you into sin, and sin separates us from God. It lures you into the place where you are vulnerable to evil and demonic oppression. It is not to be toyed with; you should only treat it with, and purge it from control over your life with, extreme prejudice.

WILLFUL SIN AND WILLING SIN CONTRASTED

Willful sin and sinning willingly, though similar in phrase, hold key distinctions that are vital to understand in the Christian walk. Intent sets the first clear difference. Willful sin involves a deliberate, conscious choice to disobey God, done with full understanding of its implications. This is not merely succumbing in a moment of weakness or ignorance; it is an intentional, knowing rebellion against God's will.

In contrast, sinning willingly may occur through lapses in judgment or temptation where the sinner does not fully embrace rebellion with hardened intent but rather struggles with their sinful nature. This is often the case for believers who love Jesus but find themselves weak in the face of temptation—wanting purity, but lacking strength to overcome by themselves.

Heart Condition further distinguishes the two. Willful sin is connected with a hardened heart, refusing repentance and deliberately rejecting Christ and His transformative power. This posture embraces the lusts of the sinful nature, setting itself against what is pure and righteous. On the other hand, sinning willingly may reflect believers who wrestle with sin but have not turned away from God; they are caught in the struggle of human weakness.

Most believers who earnestly desire Christlikeness struggle here, not out of defiance but due to infancy or immaturity in spiritual strength. The path to victory lies in growth—maturing spiritually so that the power of purity reigns, and the cravings of sin lose their grip. This growth arms believers to fight temptation not out of obligation or excuse but from a renewed desire to honor God.

The Consequences of willful sin are grave and severe in Scripture. It carries a warning of judgment and a potential state beyond forgiveness *(Hebrews 10:26–27)*, portraying a finality borne of a settled, persistent rebellion against God's grace. This leads to a state of apostasy, rejecting Christ—which is blasphemy of the Holy Spirit, whose sole purpose is to witness for Christ *(Luke 12:10)*. Yet sinning willingly—while serious—is met with grace through repentance and restoration, inviting the believer back into fellowship and purity.

Understanding these distinctions encourages believers to evaluate their heart's posture and to seek spiritual maturity. It calls for a vigilant fight fueled by the Word and Spirit, steering clear from spiritual complacency that drifts into willful rejection. Instead, walk in grace, confess sin, and pursue purity with a sincere heart empowered by God's strength.

THE SON OF GOD IN YOU AND THE SINFUL NATURE: CHOICES

The one you choose to adhere to, the one you feed, is the one that will prevail. Failure to nourish the newborn spirit of righteousness—the child of God in you—is to leave room for the growth of the sinful nature. The influence of the world acts as its food, and it abounds abundantly, especially in our current generation, which has excelled in unrighteousness far beyond previous generations.

"Dear friends, now we are children of God, and what we will be has not yet been made known. But we know that when Christ appears, we shall be like him, for we shall see him as he is. All who have this hope in him purify themselves, just as he is pure. Everyone who sins breaks the law; in fact, sin is lawlessness. But you know that he appeared so that he might take away our sins. And in him is no sin. No one who lives in him keeps on sinning. No one who continues to sin has either seen him or known him. Dear children, do not let anyone lead you astray. The one who does what is right is righteous, just as he is righteous. The one who does what is sinful is of the devil, because the devil has been sinning from the beginning. The reason the Son of God appeared was to destroy the devil's work. No one who is born of God will continue to sin, because God's seed remains in them; they cannot go on sinning, because they have been born of God. This is how we know who the children of God are and who the children of the devil are: Anyone who does not do what is right is not God's child, nor is anyone who does not love their brother and sister."
(1 John 3:2-10 NIV)

<u>THE SINFUL NATURE</u>

The sinful nature is the essence that keeps fallen man in sin. It is not a demon or an invented concept, but the direct result of humanity's fall from the Garden of Eden. As part of human nature since that fall, it is the "son of unrighteousness" within—an inherited disposition empowering Satan's influence through temptation.

Its purpose is to counter every project of righteousness in your life. It harbors unrighteousness and entices evil temptations to hinder growth in righteousness and holiness. This nature is the enemy within, ingrained into humanity's fabric from the fall.

It is a motivating craving that leads to sin—sin incarnate living within. Fed by the lusts of this fallen world, the more you indulge fleshly satisfactions, the stronger and deeper its roots take hold within your soul. It grants Satan a foothold in your life.

Yet, through salvation, a new nature is born—one that is holy, righteous, and a child of the Most High God. This new spirit frees you from slavery to sin and gives you the power to live above it. The challenge is that this new spirit starts as an infant needing growth and maturity to overpower the sinful nature and its cravings.

The sinful nature tempts continually, making sin a constant possibility unless crucified by a strong spiritual sonship. Paul's desperate cry captures this struggle: *"What a wretched man I am! Who will rescue me from this body that is subject to death?"* (Romans 7:24 NIV).

The corruption of the sinful nature is vividly depicted in Genesis: *"The LORD saw how great the wickedness of the human race had become on the earth, and that every inclination of the thoughts of the human heart was only evil all the time. The LORD regretted that he had made human beings on the earth, and his heart was deeply troubled."* (Genesis 6:5–6 NIV)

The sinful nature twists God's perfect design for our natural desires, perverting them into lust, gluttony, and other immoral indulgences that are inherently evil. Lust, especially, is demonic—warping the pure longing for intimacy into self-centered craving. Guard your sexual purity with righteous anger and ferocity; your very life depends on it. Sexual purity saves souls and nurtures redemption.

This nature thrives in idolatry and secrecy, manipulating us into addictions, strongholds, and compulsions. Therefore, do not hide your sins but expose them, confess, repent, face them, and seek fellowship and accountability. Through repentance, you begin the first step of taking back your life's territory from the darkness of sexual sin. You also in this way strip the enemy of any footholds in your life, for repentance in Christ begets freedom.

"Therefore confess your sins to each other and pray for each other so that you may be healed. The prayer of a righteous person is powerful and effective." (James 5:16 NIV) Through such openness, you begin to break the shackles of the sinful nature which create a noose around your redeemed spiritual life, trying to choke it out.

When you confess and pray, you take back control and wage the war against the misdeeds of the 'flesh' now on holy grounds and not in its territory of preference.

"Whoever conceals their sins does not prosper, but the one who confesses and renounces them finds mercy. Blessed is the one who always trembles before

God, but whoever hardens their heart falls into trouble." (Proverbs 28:13-14 NIV)

It is human nature to hide mistakes, but growth comes from acknowledgment, confession, and correction. To repeat mistakes is folly. Paul warns: *"Do not be deceived: God cannot be mocked. A man reaps what he sows. Whoever sows to please their flesh, from the flesh will reap destruction; whoever sows to please the Spirit, from the Spirit will reap eternal life."* (Galatians 6:7–8 NIV)

<u>YOU ARE SICK</u>

The sinful nature is a sickness deeply rooted in fallen humanity. It is a body of death from which Paul asks for deliverance. This internal war threatens your desire for purity and holiness. Healing requires spiritual medicine—prayer and God's Word. Without these, the disease will fester, overwhelm, and lead to spiritual defeat.

Discipline to consistently "take your medicine"—spiritual feeding through the Word of God—separates the mature from the immature. Paul reminds us: *"When I was a child, I talked like a child, I thought like a child, I reasoned like a child. When I became a man, I put the ways of childhood behind me."* (1 Corinthians 13:11 NIV) Nothing grows without nourishment. Spiritual maturity comes through diligence in prayer and Scripture.

The River of Healing

The sinful nature is a sickness within the soul—a corrosion that resists purity—therefore, healing becomes essential on the ascent toward true holiness. This healing flows from the pure waters of God, the river of life revealed in Ezekiel 47.

This river portrays the Holy Spirit Himself, cultivating divine function in the believer through the cleansing, strengthening waters of the Word. As Jesus affirmed, the Spirit speaks not from Himself but declares only what He hears from the Father—pure transmission, pure truth, pure life (*John 16:13*).

In Ezekiel's vision, led by a holy angel, he was brought outside the temple wall through the north gateway and escorted to the eastern entrance. There, he beheld water flowing from the southern side of the threshold—a stream emerging from the heart of God's dwelling.

From verse 7 onward, the angel measured out four equal segments of roughly 1,750 feet, leading Ezekiel deeper each time: ankle-deep, then knee-deep, then waist-deep, and finally waters so overwhelming that he could only swim—completely surrendered to the current.

This sacred progression unveils the stages of spiritual maturity as shaped by the Word. At the ankle level, you are like an infant—moving freely yet still vulnerable to the pull of the sinful nature. The answer is simple: advance. At the knee level, your mobility lessens; the water begins to steady and test you, though you are not yet firm. Here growth requires deeper immersion in the Scriptures. At the waist—the place of your physical center—you are half-submerged; the waters of the Word begin to challenge and subdue the sinful nature, curbing its influence and shifting your internal balance.

But the final measure pulls you beyond stability. When the waters rise above your ability to stand, you are fully carried—no longer walking by your own strength but led by the Holy Spirit. Here is victory: walking in the Spirit so that the flesh loses its grip. At this depth, the pure river of God becomes the current of your life, drawing you into the knowledge of Christ and sustaining you by grace.

These incremental measures—the repeated spans of 1,750 feet—are a metaphor that symbolizes gradual sanctification, revealing that growth is a process marked by stages: from infancy, to formation, to rootedness, and finally, total immersion—spiritual maturity and surrender.

Yet this river is not only a river of maturity; it is a river of healing. In verse 8, the angel declares that these waters flow eastward through the desert and into the Dead Sea—transforming what is lifeless, reviving what is hopeless, and making saltwater fresh. Wherever this river flows, life multiplies—even within places once considered beyond redemption.

Because of this, your growth must never be interrupted. The flow must remain continual. Verse 11 warns that marshes and swamps—areas disconnected from the flow—remain salty, unchanged, unhealed, and therefore, impure. But verse 12 promises that on both sides of this river grow trees whose leaves never wither and whose fruit never fails. Their fruit nourishes; their leaves heal—living proof of a life planted in God.

Thus, you too shall be fruitful in the kingdom of God—bearing abundant produce and growing ever richer in spiritual vitality. Paul affirms this to Timothy, saying that if one keeps oneself pure, he becomes a special utensil—clean, honorable, and ready for the Master's use in every good work (*2 Timothy 2:21*). This is the power of purity: it makes you a vessel of divine purpose, equipped to advance the culture of the Kingdom with integrity, free from the self-disqualification that impurity brings.

And notice—this river does not originate in isolation but flows from the temple. The church is the ordained source through which God releases healing into the world. Therefore, the gathering of believers is where every prudent saint must be rooted—grounded in doctrine, worship, fellowship, and the established principles of God's house. This divine order creates a stable, abundant, and continual flow.

Such waters cannot be accessed alone; they are released through the corporate grace of the church. They flow through sermons, fellowship, worship, and every measure of God's servants. As you remain submerged in this river, you mature, you are healed, and eventually, you overflow with thankfulness—carried not by your might but by the Spirit of the Living God. And as these waters heal you, they begin to flow through you—bringing healing to others and breaking the dominion of the sinful nature wherever the river extends.

THE SINFUL NATURE HAS MEANS THAT END IN SIN

God confronted Cain saying: *"Why are you angry? Why is your face downcast? If you do what is right, will you not be accepted? But if you do not do what is right, sin is crouching at your door; it desires to have you, but you must rule over it."* (Genesis 4:6–7 NIV) Sin crouches at the door, desiring to have you, but it can only enter if you invite it. Emotions like anger, depression, anxiety, and lust can open the door to deeper bondage. They act as triggers.

Do not answer the door to sin's knocking. The devil seeks footholds to rule over your life. Strength and discernment are needed to break these strongholds, but prevention is best. Isaiah commands: *"Awake, awake, Zion, clothe yourself with strength! Put on your garments of splendor, Jerusalem, the holy city. The uncircumcised and defiled will not enter you again."* (Isaiah

52:1 NIV) Clothe yourself with strength; do not let the sinful nature triumph again.

CRUCIFYING THE SINFUL NATURE

"T hose who belong to Christ Jesus have crucified the flesh with its passions and desires." (Galatians 5:24 NIV)

'SARX': ITS CRUCIFIXION!

The sinful nature must be put to death. Otherwise, seeking to live a life of righteousness becomes an impossibility where it still controls and exercises power over you. Its cords must be severed from the command center of your life—your mind. It is paramount that every child of God reaches the place of spiritual maturity where the lures of the sinful nature hold no grasp.

This is the realm of freedom where you no longer carry an innate desire or sense of obligation to gratify the flesh. Here, you find yourself able to live righteously without the fear of falling back into sin or rekindling the life of the sinful nature.

Romans 8:5–9 declares: *"Those who live according to the flesh have their minds set on what the flesh desires; but those who live in accordance with the*

Spirit have their minds set on what the Spirit desires. The mind governed by the flesh is death, but the mind governed by the Spirit is life and peace. The mind governed by the flesh is hostile to God; it does not submit to God's law, nor can it do so. Those who are in the realm of the flesh cannot please God. You, however, are not in the realm of the flesh but are in the realm of the Spirit, if indeed the Spirit of God lives in you. And if anyone does not have the Spirit of Christ, they do not belong to Christ." (NIV)

To live according to the Holy Spirit is to stand firmly on the Word of God, continually feeding your spirit. In doing so, you align your mind with the desires of the Spirit. But if you neglect continual spiritual nourishment—if you do not feed the child of God within—you will inevitably live according to the sinful nature, regardless of your intentions.

In such a weakened state, the desires of the flesh dominate your outlook and actions. Therefore, feed the inner child of God so the Holy Spirit may mature your being, producing a stable, consistent purity.

Consider this: if you do not feed your physical body, it deteriorates, immunity fails, and sickness and frailty begin to overtake you. Likewise, when you fail to feed your spirit—born through faith in Christ by the Holy Spirit—your spirit becomes faint, lacking the immunity needed to resist the "disease" of the sinful nature.

Eventually, you risk spiritual death and drift down the path of unrighteousness, as the corruption of the sinful nature continues to fester and lead you deeper into evil.

Galatians 5:19-23 teaches: *"The acts of the flesh are obvious: sexual immorality, impurity and debauchery; idolatry and witchcraft; hatred, discord, jealousy, fits of rage, selfish ambition, dissensions, factions and envy;*

drunkenness, orgies, and the like. I warn you, as I did before, that those who live like this will not inherit the kingdom of God. But the fruit of the Spirit is love, joy, peace, forbearance, kindness, goodness, faithfulness, gentleness and self-control. Against such things there is no law." (NIV)

If you do not live by the Spirit, only the sinful nature remains—and the sinful nature never needs your permission to rule you. It becomes the default controlling force. Its desires are evil, manifesting as sexual immorality, impurity, lust, idolatry, hatred, jealousy, anger, selfish ambition, dissension, drunkenness, and countless others.

With each generation, the lusts of the flesh escalate, inventing further perversions and new ways to gratify themselves, pulling humanity further from God. Sin always separates us from His presence, but the Holy Spirit leads us toward maturity, empowering us to reject the rising tide of immorality and embrace the freedom of righteousness.

The will of the Holy Spirit and the desires of the sinful nature stand in constant opposition—one producing death, the other life. The contrast is unmistakable: the sinful nature leads to destruction, bondage, and moral decay, while the fruit of the Spirit is productive, holy, life-giving, and sustaining—love, joy, peace, and much more. Triumphant living does not arise from human effort but from yielding to the Holy Spirit and the Word of God, the only source of true victory.

AN ALLEGORY OF TRANSFORMATION

Just as in the beginning the earth was formless and empty, with darkness covering the deep, the Spirit of God hovered over the waters. When God spoke, *"Let there be..."*, beauty and order were created through the power of His Word and Spirit *(Genesis 1:2–3)*. Likewise, when your life is covered by the "waters" of the Word, the Holy Spirit hovers over you. Then, when God speaks, purity is birthed within you.

As Jeremiah 29:11 assures: *"For I know the plans I have for you,' declares the LORD, 'plans to prosper you and not to harm you, plans to give you hope and a future.'" (NIV)* This transformation is only possible when your life is permeated by the Word and the Spirit, enabling true spiritual growth and purity.

"Let your roots grow down into him, and let your lives be built on him. Then your faith will grow strong in the truth you were taught, and you will overflow with thankfulness." (Colossians 2:7 NLT) This speaks of the unseen work of spiritual anchoring. Roots are not decorative—they are the hidden strength of a tree.

Likewise, your purity cannot be external performance or momentary zeal. Your spirit must grow roots downward into Christ, drawing nourishment from His Word until your entire life is constructed upon Him. In this posture, faith becomes fortified; truth becomes internalized; thankfulness becomes the overflow of a life grounded in stability.

Purity rises not because you strive but because your roots drink from Christ Himself. A rooted believer cannot be easily uprooted by temptation, nor swayed by the winds of the sinful nature. Strength in the secret place becomes victory in the visible life.

"When you came to Christ, you were "circumcised," but not by physical procedure. Christ performed a spiritual circumcision—the cutting away of your sinful nature. (Colossians 2:11 NLT) Here lies the decisive act of Christ upon your inner being. This circumcision is not of skin but of

nature—an operation performed by the Spirit. In salvation, Christ cuts away the authority of the sinful nature, dethroning its claim over your life.

What once ruled you is now rendered powerless to command obedience. This is not symbolic; it is spiritual surgery. To walk in purity is to live consciously aware that the old ruler has been removed. The sinful nature survives only where it is fed; it thrives only where the believer remains ignorant of this divine circumcision. But in Christ, the old governance is "put off"—the Spirit establishes a new rule, a new appetite, and a new identity clothed in righteousness.

"He canceled the record of the charges against us and took it away by nailing it to the cross. In this way, he disarmed the spiritual rulers and authorities. He shamed them publicly by his victory over them on the cross." (Colossians 2:14–15 NLT) These verses unveil the cosmic dimension of purity. The cross was not merely forgiveness—it was conquest. Every accusation, every stain of sin, every demonic legal claim was nailed to the cross and forever annulled.

Through that act, Christ disarmed the rulers and authorities—the spiritual forces that once enforced the power of the sinful nature. Their weapons were stripped, their influence broken, and their victory shattered publicly. Purity is not lived from a place of fear but from triumph. You rise not as one barely escaping sin, but as one standing on the ground Christ already conquered. Your purity is upheld by His victory, not your struggle. The cross removes condemnation and empowers transformation.

"Since you died with Christ to the elemental spiritual forces of this world, why, as though you still belonged to the world, do you submit to its rules" (Colossians 2:20 NIV) This is the rebuke and awakening call. If you died

with Christ, then the world no longer defines you, controls you, or dictates your behavior.

The elemental forces—the spiritual systems, cultural currents, and fleshly impulses—no longer have jurisdiction over the believer. To submit again to their rules is to live beneath your spiritual stature, to act as though the cross never occurred.

Purity requires agreement with your death in Christ. If you died to the old life, why live as though it still governs you? Rise above the gravity of the world. Walk in the authority of the Spirit. Refuse to bow to the decrees of a nature that no longer owns you. You were raised to a higher plane—live there.

Growing in the Word establishes your roots deep in Christ, removing the power base of the sinful nature. In this stature of spiritual maturity, Christ's victory becomes your lived reality—not merely a lofty revelation—cutting off the sinful nature at its root.

"God paid a high price for you, so don't be enslaved by the world." (1 Corinthians 7:23 NLT) Do not allow yourself to be enslaved to the world or influenced by those still governed by the sinful nature. Christ purchased your freedom with His blood—live in that liberty.

A REVELATION OF SALVATION

To comprehend the magnitude of salvation—freedom from sin's power—realize that God is not bound by time. *"In the beginning God created the heavens and the earth."* (Genesis 1:1 NIV) God made time, space, and matter, existing completely outside them. When you were saved, the Holy

Spirit—unbound by the limitations that govern the created order—immersed you into Christ's crucifixion, so you died to sinful nature.

In God's eternal sight, the moment you believed, you were placed into the victory of the Cross as though physically present at Calvary. This means that salvation is not merely a moral adjustment or a spiritual improvement; it is a death and resurrection reality. You are called not to revisit or resurrect the life you died to, but to walk in the fullness purchased for you, the fullness sealed in the timeless work of Christ.

"For you died to this life, and your real life is hidden with Christ in God. ⁴ And when Christ, who is your life, is revealed to the whole world, you will share in all his glory. So put to death the sinful, earthly things lurking within you. Have nothing to do with sexual immorality, impurity, lust, and evil desires. Don't be greedy, for a greedy person is an idolater, worshiping the things of this world... Don't lie to each other, for you have stripped off your old sinful nature and all its wicked deeds. Put on your new nature, and be renewed as you learn to know your Creator and become like him. In this new life, it doesn't matter if you are a Jew or a Gentile, circumcised or uncircumcised, barbaric, uncivilized, slave, or free. Christ is all that matters, and he lives in all of us." (Colossians 3:3–5, 9–11 NLT)

This passage reveals the divine sequence: identity first, responsibility second. Because you died, you must now *put to death* the earthly nature—not by human striving but by living from the reality of your hidden life in Christ. The command is rooted in who you have become.

"Therefore, if anyone is in Christ, the new creation has come: The old has gone, the new is here!" (2 Corinthians 5:17 NIV) Salvation is not cosmetic; it is creative. A new nature is birthed, but it must be continually put on as you grow. This is why Scripture declares, *"Rather, clothe yourselves with*

the Lord Jesus Christ, and do not think about how to gratify the desires of the flesh." (Romans 13:14 NIV)

Clothing yourself with Christ is the daily embrace of the new creation life—an intentional submission to the Spirit's work until your mind, appetites, and lifestyle align with your regenerated identity.

Jesus illustrated this journey of maturity to Peter: *"'Very truly I tell you, when you were younger you dressed yourself and went where you wanted; but when you are old you will stretch out your hands, and someone else will dress you and lead you where you do not want to go.'"* (John 21:18 NIV)

The young in Christ move by impulse; the mature are governed by surrender. The Spirit is the one that leads the mature to the place the flesh does not want to go—the place of its crucifixion. Spiritual maturity is measured by yieldedness over time, not just years spent in church.

The Call to Sanctification

"It is God's will that you should be sanctified: that you should avoid sexual immorality." (1 Thessalonians 4:3 NIV) Sanctification is not optional; it is the expressed will of God for every believer. Sexual purity is not merely refraining from sexual sin—it is a consecrated lifestyle that honors God in body, mind, and spirit. Purity is not restrictive; it is protective. It separates you from the corruption of the world and aligns you with the nature of Christ within.

Scripture continues: *"May God Himself, the God of peace, sanctify you through and through. May your whole spirit, soul and body be kept blameless at the coming of our Lord Jesus Christ. The one who calls you is faithful, and He will do it."* (1 Thessalonians 5:23–24 NIV)

Sanctification is comprehensive and divine in origin. It touches spirit *(the Godward part of you)*, soul *(your mind, will, and emotions)*, and body *(your conduct and physical habits)*. Holiness is not achieved by human resilience but by divine faithfulness. God does not merely command purity—He performs purity in the yielded believer.

Pursuit, Fellowship, And Spiritual Sharpening

"Run from anything that stimulates youthful lusts. Instead, pursue righteous living, faithfulness, love, and peace. Enjoy the companionship of those who call on the Lord with pure hearts." (2 Timothy 2:22 NLT) Purity is both escape and pursuit.

Fleeing temptation alone is insufficient unless replaced by running toward righteousness. And this pursuit thrives in community—*with those* whose hearts are also pure. Purity flourishes through shared devotion, accountability, and spiritual companionship.

This is why Scripture anchors community so strongly: *"Not giving up meeting together, as some are in the habit of doing, but encouraging one another—and all the more as you see the Day approaching."* (Hebrews 10:25 NIV) Isolation is dangerous to purity; fellowship fortifies it. *"As iron sharpens iron, so one person sharpens another."* (Proverbs 27:17 NIV) Sharpening is intentional friction—the holy refinement that occurs when believers walk closely together in truth and love.

The Freedom and Responsibility in Grace

"Therefore, there is now no condemnation for those who are in Christ Jesus." (Romans 8:1 NIV) Purity cannot grow in the soil of condemnation. The devil uses shame to trap believers in cycles of defeat, but God uses grace to

empower transformation. The absence of condemnation is not permission for sin but liberation from the guilt that fuels sin. The believer who truly grasps this walks in the strength of grace rather than the fear of failure.

"Let us go right into the presence of God with sincere hearts fully trusting him. For our guilty consciences have been sprinkled with Christ's blood to make us clean, and our bodies have been washed with pure water." (Hebrews 10:22 NLT) Purity is sustained by communion with God, where conscience is cleansed and the inward man renewed. Purity begins in the heart and manifests in conduct.

The Word of God plays a central role: *"All Scripture is God-breathed and is useful for teaching, rebuking, correcting and training in righteousness, so that the servant of God may be thoroughly equipped for every good work."* (2 Timothy 3:16–17 NIV) Without the Word, the believer is under-equipped—vulnerable to deception, error, and spiritual weakness. Scripture trains the soul in righteousness until the inner life aligns with divine truth.

"Physical training is good, but training for godliness is much better, promising benefits in this life and in the life to come." (1 Timothy 4:8 NLT) Spiritual discipline surpasses physical discipline because it strengthens the eternal man. Godliness produces purity, clarity, strength, and spiritual stature.

The Necessity of Internalization

Ezekiel is our witness. Only when he internalized the words of God, was he authorized to minister to Israel: *"Then he added, 'Son of man, let all my words sink deep into your own heart first. Listen to them carefully for yourself. Then go to your people...'"* (Ezekiel 3:10-11 NLT) Purity requires this depth—God's Word must settle into the heart before it can flow out in power. No one can walk in sustained holiness without internalizing divine truth.

This Word is eternal and unchanging: *"Heaven and earth will pass away, but my words will never pass away."* (Matthew 24:35 NIV) *"The grass withers and the flowers fall, but the word of our God endures forever."* (Isaiah 40:8 NIV) Purity stands firm when anchored in the eternal Word.

The New Birth and The Mirror of Obedience

"For you have been born again, not of perishable seed, but of imperishable, through the living and enduring word of God." (1 Peter 1:23 NIV) Purity begins with the seed of the Word that birthed you. Imperishable seed produces imperishable life—holy, incorruptible, aligned with God's nature.

But purity must be practiced: *"For if you listen to the word and don't obey, it is like glancing at your face in a mirror. You see yourself, walk away, and forget what you look like. But if you look carefully into the perfect law that sets you free, and if you do what it says and don't forget what you heard, then God will bless you for doing it."* (James 1:23–25 NLT) The Word reveals identity, but obedience preserves identity. Transformation requires continuation, not momentary inspiration.

The Promise of Seeing God

"Blessed are the pure in heart, for they will see God." (Matthew 5:8 NIV) Purity is not simply the avoidance of sin; it is the progressive unveiling of God to the consecrated heart. The pure see God in His ways, His movements, His voice, His dealings. Purity is the pathway to revelation.

This is the indispensable role of God's Word, community, and the Spirit in maturing into a life of purity. Feeding the spirit, fleeing youthful lusts, embracing fellowship, and pressing into godliness are not mere ideals but essential pathways empowered by God's enduring promises. Purity is possible because God is faithful. It rises from above, wrought in the believer by the eternal Word, the sanctifying Spirit, and the crucified Christ.

THE IMPORTANCE OF MATURITY IN THE PURSUIT OF PURITY

Paul's words in *Galatians 4:1–7* frame our spiritual journey as a process of divine maturation. Though an heir legally owns the entire estate, he is no different from a slave while he remains a child. He is placed under guardians and trustees until the appointed time set by the Father.

Likewise, before Christ came, we were all held in bondage under the elemental principles of this fallen world. But when the fullness of time arrived, God sent His Son—born of a woman, born under the law—to redeem us, that we might receive adoption into sonship. And because we are sons, God sent the Spirit of His Son into our hearts, crying, *"Abba, Father."* We are no longer slaves but sons—and as sons, heirs of God Himself *(Galatians 4:1–7).*

If you do not grow in your salvation, you remain bound, still functioning as one enslaved under the principles of the world. Sin and temptation will continue to crouch at your door, eager to reign over you. True freedom is attained only by ascending the mountain of God—a journey of increasing intimacy, deepening revelation, and continual spiritual growth. This ascent is maturity. *(1 Peter 2:2)*

The measure of your spiritual maturity shapes the longevity, stability, and depth of your relationship with God. Where maturity is lacking, discord will arise—not only in your human relationships but most painfully in your walk with God. The rampant sin seen in the Church today is itself a witness to widespread spiritual infancy.

Paul's evaluation of the Corinthian church exposes this condition: he could not address them as people who live by the Spirit but as those who are still worldly—mere infants in Christ. He fed them with spiritual milk, for solid food was beyond their capacity.

Their jealousy, quarrelling, and divisiveness revealed their immaturity; they behaved like mere humans, not Spirit-formed believers *(1 Corinthians 3:1–3)*. Again, in his second letter, he calls them to rise: *"Be joyful. Grow to maturity. Encourage each other. Live in harmony and peace. Then the God of love and peace will be with you."* (2 Corinthians 13:11 NLT)

Without spiritual maturity, purity remains unreachable. Maturity is the fortified wall around the soul that guards against the intrusion of sin. Proverbs declares, *"Like a city whose walls are broken through is a person who lacks self-control."* (Proverbs 25:28 NIV)

When self-control is absent, the defenses of the soul collapse, leaving the believer vulnerable to every assault of the flesh. Your degree of spiritual maturity determines your capacity for restraint, discernment, and victory.

Grow in Christ; become self-controlled. For only the mature can steward purity, sustain purity, and walk in the fullness of the life God has already appointed for them.

<u>FREEDOM IN CHRIST: THE LOVE OF GOD FOR MATURITY</u>

"It is for freedom that Christ has set us free. Stand firm, then, and do not let yourselves be burdened again by a yoke of slavery." (Galatians 5:1 NIV)

Christ set you free at a high and holy cost; therefore, do not return to the chains of human regulations or the cravings of the sinful nature. Freedom is not merely the absence of bondage but the grace-empowered capacity to live above the gravitational pull of the flesh. You were liberated to ascend, not to descend; redeemed to walk in sonship, not slavery.

Paul continues with a warning that exposes the true purpose of freedom: *"You, my brothers and sisters, were called to be free. But do not use your freedom to indulge the flesh; rather, serve one another humbly in love."* (Galatians 5:13 NIV)

Freedom is not a license for indulgence. It is an invitation to love. When freedom is divorced from love, it collapses into sin. When joined to love, it blossoms into righteousness. If we persist in sin after receiving salvation, no ritual or offering can cleanse what we 'willfully' choose to indulge. True freedom expresses itself through the love that Christ births in the heart, compelling us toward holiness.

Paul's portrait of love in 1 Corinthians 13 unmasks the shallow loves of this age and reveals the essence of true maturity: *"Love is patient, love is kind. It does not envy, it does not boast, it is not proud. It does not dishonor others, it is not self-seeking, it is not easily angered, it keeps no record of wrongs."* (1 Corinthians 13:4–5 NIV)

Sexual immorality and impurity are proofs of a heart devoid of true love. For love does not devour; it protects. Love does not seek self-gratification;

it seeks the well-being of others. When Christ's love governs you, lust loses its voice. The pursuit of purity is never sustained by discipline alone—it is anchored in love matured by the Spirit.

The story of Joseph stands as a living witness of this truth. Confronted with relentless temptation, he fled youthful lusts and held fast to righteousness, proving that integrity is the foundation of authority. Scripture commands likewise: *"Flee the evil desires of youth and pursue righteousness, faith, love and peace, along with those who call on the Lord out of a pure heart."* (2 Timothy 2:22 NIV)

Love and spiritual maturity walk hand in hand, ascending together toward purity that rises from above. Paul's prayer captures this holy progression:

"I pray that your love will overflow more and more, and that you will keep on growing in knowledge and understanding. For I want you to understand what really matters, so that you may live pure and blameless lives until the day of Christ's return. May you always be filled with the fruit of your salvation—the righteous character produced in your life by Jesus Christ—for this will bring much glory and praise to God." (Philippians 1:9–11 NLT)

This growth in love and discernment is not powered by emotion but by revelation—by the knowledge of Christ and the weight of His mission upon your life. When knowledge fuels love, and love empowers obedience, spiritual maturity is ignited. And from that flame, purity ascends—holy, steady, and victorious.

<u>THERE IS NO ADVANCEMENT IN FAITH WITHOUT SPIRITUAL MATURITY</u>

Hebrews confronts the sobering reality that spiritual stagnation cripples advancement in the faith.

"We have much to say about this, but it is hard to make it clear to you because you no longer try to understand. In fact, though by this time you ought to be teachers, you need someone to teach you the elementary truths of God's word all over again. You need milk, not solid food! Anyone who lives on milk, being still an infant, is not acquainted with the teaching about righteousness. But solid food is for the mature, who by constant use have trained themselves to distinguish good from evil."(Hebrews 5:11–14 NIV)

Immaturity dulls spiritual perception. It leaves the believer unacquainted with righteousness, untrained in discernment, and unable to handle the deeper truths of God. Maturity, however, is forged by constant use—through obedience, application, and steadfast pursuit of God's ways. Only the mature can distinguish good from evil; only the mature can advance.

From the unifying love of Christ, the entire Church is held together. The graces operating through apostles, prophets, evangelists, pastors, and teachers exist for one divine purpose: to equip the saints with the Word of God so that every believer may be built up, strengthened, and brought into maturity. Paul captures this holy mandate:

"This will continue until we all come to such unity in our faith and knowledge of God's Son that we will be mature in the Lord, measuring up to the full and complete standard of Christ. Then we will no longer be immature like children. We won't be tossed and blown about by every wind of new teaching.

We will not be influenced when people try to trick us with lies so clever they sound like the truth. Instead, we will speak the truth in love, growing in every way more and more like Christ, who is the head of His body, the Church." (Ephesians 4:13–15 NLT)

Maturity is the fruit of unity in faith and knowledge. It is the stature of Christ formed within the believer—a depth of grounding that prevents deception, stabilizes the soul, and empowers truth spoken in love. Maturity goes beyond information; it is the ability to discern, remain rooted, and respond in Christlike integrity.

If you neglect growth in salvation, you remain bound beneath the corrupting elements of this fallen world. Sin lurks. Temptation crouches. Worldly pressures whisper. Without maturity, these forces keep you ensnared. To break free, one must ascend the mountain of God—drawing nearer, going deeper, submitting further. This ascent is not merely devotion; it is the very formation of maturity. For only the mature rise above, and only the mature walk in the purity that descends from heaven and rises within. In short, 'Purity Rises from Maturity!'

CONTENDING FOR PURITY: THE BATTLE FOR RIGHTEOUSNESS

Growing into maturity is not a passive unfolding but an intentional ascent. Strength must be wielded, not merely possessed. You take that strength to the battlefield of the mind, lifting the sword of the Spirit—which is the Word of God—against every impulse that seeks to drag you back into impurity.

The sinful nature is never solitary in its assault. It collaborates with the forces of darkness, working to weaken your resolve, corrupt your integrity, and hinder your rise into the deep things of God.

As we have already established, the sinful nature is the internal abode of evil. It facilitates darkness, creating an environment where the enemy plants footholds—weights that burden your soul, slow your pace, and resist your spiritual acceleration in this race of life.

The kingdom of darkness amplifies its influence through demonic engagement, exploiting every unyielded place within you. Yet the Holy Spirit is infinitely more powerful than the sinful nature. The danger lies not in His insufficiency but in our misplaced confidence. When we rely on our own wisdom, we choose wrongly. When we attempt to follow the Spirit through human effort alone, we collapse under the weight of our limitations.

Our singular pathway to freedom is full surrender. Only by empowering the Holy Spirit—yielding every desire, every thought, every secret chamber of the heart—can we overthrow the evil inclinations lurking within. This empowerment flows through edification found exclusively in Him and through His Word.

Only then can we contend for purity: not merely resisting the sinful nature within, but standing firm against the demonic strategies without—against the dark powers that aim to weaponize your flesh, sabotage your ascent, and keep you from becoming what God ordained in the fullness of purity.

THE BATTLEFIELD OF THE MIND

The mind is the first theater of war, for the sinful nature is not self-sustaining—it is funded by Satan himself. Scripture lays bare the depth of humanity's fallen condition:

"Once you were dead because of your disobedience and your many sins. You used to live in sin, just like the rest of the world, obeying the devil—the commander of the powers in the unseen world. He is the spirit at work in the hearts of those who refuse to obey God. All of us used to live that way, following the passionate desires and inclinations of our sinful nature. By our very nature, we were subject to God's anger, just like everyone else. But God is so rich in mercy, and He loved us so much, that even though we were dead because of our sins, He gave us life when He raised Christ from the dead. (It is only by God's grace that you have been saved!) For He raised us from the dead along with Christ and seated us with Him in the heavenly realms because we are united with Christ Jesus." (Ephesians 2:1–6 NLT)

This passage reveals a profound truth: the sinful nature is a conduit for satanic influence. Through it, the enemy seeks to shape desires, manipulate thoughts, and steer actions away from God.

Recognizing this is vital, for the call to *"put off"* the old nature and *"put on"* the new (Ephesians 4:22–24) is not merely an act of personal discipline but an engagement in spiritual warfare. As the Spirit renews your mind, you confront not only internal corruption but also external powers intent on sabotaging your progress in purity.

"You were taught, with regard to your former way of life, to put off your old self, which is being corrupted by its deceitful desires; to be made new in the

attitude of your minds; and to put on the new self, created to be like God in true righteousness and holiness." (Ephesians 4:22–24 NIV)

Victory over the sinful nature is never isolated from God's divine equipping. Redemption is not merely the salvation of humanity but the revelation of God's wisdom to the unseen realms: *"God's purpose in all this was to use the church to display his wisdom in its rich variety to all the rulers and authorities in the heavenly places."* (Ephesians 3:10 NLT)

This victory requires fervent, consistent prayer—your lifeline to divine strength and clarity. *"...The prayer of a righteous person is powerful and effective."* (James 5:16 NIV)

Prayer, joined to the Word, fortifies the inner man. It sharpens your spirit, strengthens your authority, and equips you to withstand and overthrow every influence seeking to pull you back into bondage. For this reason, God has provided the full armor of God—because purity must be defended, righteousness must be contended for, and victory must be enforced.

THE ARMOR OF GOD: WEAPONS OF THE WORD

"Finally, be strong in the Lord and in his mighty power..." (Ephesians 6:10–18 NIV) forms the divine foundation for spiritual warfare. The call to *put on the full armor of God* is not a poetic metaphor—it is a command, a survival strategy, and a blueprint for victory against the schemes of the devil.

Our struggle is not human; it is spiritual. We war against rulers, authorities, powers of this dark world, and spiritual forces of evil in the heavenly realms. Thus, God equips us with armor forged from His Word so that when the day of adversity comes, we may stand firm, unshaken, unmoved.

Each piece of this armor corresponds directly to the Word of God. The **Belt of Truth** fastens your life to what is eternal and unchanging: *"Sanctify them by the truth; your word is truth."* (John 17:17 NIV)

The **Breastplate of Righteousness** shields your heart as you walk in obedience: *"Blessed are those whose ways are blameless, who walk according to the law of the LORD."* (Psalm 119:1 NIV)

The **Shoes of the Gospel** anchor your steps in the message of Christ's salvation—the Word that brings peace. The **Shield of Faith** extinguishes every flaming arrow of the enemy, for: *"Faith comes from hearing the message, and the message is heard through the word about Christ."* (Romans 10:17 NIV)

The **Helmet of Salvation** guards your mind, securing the assurance we receive by trusting the Good News: *"For it is by grace you have been saved, through faith—and this is not from yourselves, it is the gift of God."* (Ephesians 2:8 NIV)

And the **Sword of the Spirit**—our only offensive weapon—is the Word made alive and active, cutting through darkness with divine precision: *"For the word of God is alive and active. Sharper than any double-edged sword, it penetrates even to dividing soul and spirit, joints and marrow; it judges the thoughts and attitudes of the heart."* (Hebrews 4:12 NIV)

Clothed in these weapons drawn from Scripture, mature believers stand ready. Armored in truth, righteousness, faith, peace, salvation, and the living Word, you can face every force of darkness with unwavering resolve—victory is assured.

"For our struggle is not against flesh and blood, but against the rulers, against the authorities, against the powers of this dark world and against the spiritual forces of evil in the heavenly realms." Ephesians 6:12 NIV, reaffirms the reality of our adversaries. These rulers and authorities are not symbolic—they are demons under the command of Satan, actively working to destroy the Church of Christ.

Scripture does not soften this truth; it exposes it. Their mission is to turn hearts back into sin, for the sinful nature is the platform upon which they operate, corrupt, and restrain the believer's ascent.

Though Christ has already triumphed over the entire kingdom of darkness, our engagement in the battle continues until He returns. The devil wars relentlessly, and therefore we must stand relentlessly.

Spiritual resistance is not seasonal—it is continual. Because of this ceaseless conflict, we require supernatural empowerment to subdue spiritual foes. Thus, God clothes us with His armor, all rooted in His mighty Word.

He has given us the Holy Spirit—the Teacher promised by Christ—who equips us through the Word, strengthens our inner man, and trains our hands for war: *"But when the Father sends the Advocate as my representative—that is, the Holy Spirit—he will teach you everything and will remind you of everything I have told you."* (John 14:26, NLT)

And if discouragement ever rises, let this unshakable declaration anchor your soul: *"...Upon this rock I will build my Church, and all the powers of hell will not conquer it."* (Matthew 16:18 NLT)

The battle is fierce, but Christ's victory is final. Stand firm. The armor is yours. The Spirit is within you. The Word is your weapon. And purity—fiercely contended for—will rise from above.

CONTENDING WITH GENERATIONAL PATTERNS OF SEXUAL IMMORALITY

Purity is also called to confront generational sin—patterns and curses of sexual immorality that devastate families and communities. As new creations, believers must sever these chains through the power of Jesus' blood and prayer. If not, impurities will persist across generations, threatening societal foundations.

Sexual immorality extends beyond individual sin; it is a weapon of the enemy to destroy communities before they even come to be. This explains why sexuality—one of the three main pillars of human society—is fiercely attacked by darkness. The thief comes only to steal, kill, and destroy, leveraging sexual sin to perpetuate destruction across time.

David's sin with Bathsheba stands as a sobering example of this destructive domino effect. Having finally become king, sharing in the victories and power, David grew lax in his fervor and dedication to God. When kings marched forth to war, David sent his commander out instead, choosing to remain behind—a decision that opened the door to temptation. When he saw Bathsheba bathing, lust seized his heart, leading to sin that could have been avoided by vigilance and consecration. *(2 Samuel 11,12)*

As the prophet Nathan foretold, destruction befell David's family. Rebellion and sexual immorality spread: his daughter Tamar was violated by her half-brother Amnon, who was later killed by Tamar's brother Absalom. Absalom's subsequent rebellion further tore the family apart.

Finally, Absalom continued on to publicly defame him by sleeping with his concubines in the sight of all Israel on top of the palace roof. *(2 Samuel 13, 16)*.

This tragic sequence illustrates how sexual sin fractures families—the basic building blocks of society—and threatens the very pillar of sexuality that upholds civilization. Sexual sin is no private indulgence but a destructive force demanding sanctification for the sake of all generations.

Allegory of purity in the current floods of immorality: Build an Ark of Righteousness—an ark of purity. As the floods of destruction rise to consume the rest of your generation, you will rise higher as Noah's ark rose above the waters, shielding your own posterity and those who follow you, those God has entrusted to the sphere of your influence. For without sexual purity, lives and callings are jeopardized, forfeited, and destroyed.

<u>DO NOT ENTERTAIN THE TRAVELER</u>

In *2 Samuel 12:1–4*, Nathan tells David a parable:

"There were two men in a certain town, one rich and the other poor. The rich man had a very large number of sheep and cattle, but the poor man had nothing except one little ewe lamb he had bought. He raised it, and it grew up with him and his children. It shared his food, drank from his cup and even slept in his arms. It was like a daughter to him. Now a traveler came to the rich man, but the rich man refrained from taking one of his own sheep or cattle to prepare a meal for the traveler who had come to him. Instead, he took the ewe lamb that belonged to the poor man and prepared it for the one who had come to him." (2 Samuel 12:1–4 NIV)

The "traveler" symbolizes an evil and destructive spirit appearing as a thought. The battlefield for your purity is your mind. As with David, an idle mind welcomes the traveler, planting seeds that lead to unrighteous acts—sometimes subtle but always dangerous. Vigilance and spiritual discipline guard the gates of your mind to preserve purity.

Dosage that keeps him at bay is found in *Philippians 4:8* and *Galatians 5:22–23*: good thoughts and the fruits of the Holy Spirit. We ought to be vigilant always. Bring every thought captive. Fight him in prayer. Destroy his power by constantly waging war against the flesh nature that gives him a platform.

The spirit man must always be stronger in you if you are to live above gratifying the desires of the sinful nature which he cultivates passionately. You can keep him out of the household of your being. Understand that compromising the potency of the pesticide you have against this pest means it will fester and eventually consume your hard-earned leverage, as it did with David.

Your life is a field that must bear the fruits of righteousness—the fruits of the Holy Spirit. This pest requires you to be a vigilant farmer in that field. The traveler comes from underground—that is, through the sinful nature which innately resides in the fabric of human nature, within the very field you labor to cultivate.

To purge the field of your life from the misdeeds of the sinful nature, not only must the flesh be put to death, but the traveler, too, must be combated and overcome.

If you compromise the potency of your prayer life or your relationship of constant communion with the Holy Spirit through growing in the

Word of God, the traveler will surely return to test the field. He is always watching from afar, waiting for an opportune moment when the farmer chooses to sleep instead of work. *"Watch and pray so that you will not fall into temptation. The spirit is willing, but the flesh is weak."* (Matthew 26:41, NIV)

When Satan left Jesus after tempting Him, Scripture says he left "until an opportune time." *"When the devil had finished all this tempting, he left him until an opportune time."* (Luke 4:13 NIV) If you are not strong in the LORD and guarded by a mature spiritual life in Christ by the time that opportune moment arrives, you will be overcome yet again.

The traveler aims to destroy you when you are near harvest time or when you are at peak level. He comes even when you are out of season, as he did with David. If the farmer is not organized, the traveler finds a loophole. He sends thoughts and desires—a mere suggestion, a foretaste—and then watches intently to see if the sinful nature in you is still alive, still in control, or still strong enough to take the bait. Do not entertain anything of him.

If you find a trigger or pitfall of temptation that this pest uses, demolish it from the field of your life once and for all, and establish strict boundaries to shield yourself. Plant something in its place: the seed of the Word of God, the fellowship of the saints, the teaching of the Word, meditation on the Word, and prayer. Set and honor your boundaries. (In the next chapter, we will explore boundaries in depth.)

The traveler destroys—contaminates—the field where your crops grow. If you do not contend for the field's integrity, its purity, the pestilence will consume the field to your detriment and the demise of your fervor for Christ. We must all fight the traveler. We must all encounter him. He is "temptation through thoughts." It is not a sin to be tempted; Jesus was tempted. It is a sin, however, to entertain the temptation and its source, and then succumb to it.

Like Jesus, we combat the tempter with the pure, holy, powerful, mighty-to-save Word of God. Temptation is the traveler peeping into your house, but sin is when you let him in.

Demolish the attempts of the tempter—the vain thoughts, temptations, and arguments that try to coddle the presence of sin. Destroy their multitudes. When you give in to his lustful thoughts sent to entice the sinful nature, it ends in lustful actions, and the pestilence festers further.

Sinful actions may be more dangerous than sinful thoughts, but sinful thoughts are the source of these actions and are just as detrimental to individual righteousness as the acts themselves. So that you are not turned away from God, these thoughts and mental arguments must be demolished.

"We demolish arguments and every pretension that sets itself up against the knowledge of God, and we take captive every thought to make it obedient to Christ." (2 Corinthians 10:5, NIV)It is a constant battle between the spirit and the flesh, and we cannot afford to lose. We have hope of relief in the future when our Lord and Savior Jesus Christ returns and destroys the works of Satan, but understand: now is not the time to reminisce or grow lax because we have grace.

Now is the time to use that grace to resist the devil, submit to God, and watch the enemy flee. *"Submit yourselves, then, to God. Resist the devil, and he will flee from you."* (James 4:7, NIV)

When the traveler comes, the farmer has a choice—either to allow his presence and entertain him, or to chase him away. David chose the former.

Learn from his mistake and do not repeat the pattern. The Traveler, being an evil spirit and a visiting guest in Nathan's parable, always requires a sacrifice from you—something of your substance to devour.

The tempter will never ask for anything good but will seek what destroys your integrity, purity, and reputation. He entices and awakens the diseased substance buried in your field—the sinful nature, which must be put to death. As with David, he will cause evil in your domain by provoking the sinful nature's desire for compromise.

"I strike a blow to my body and make it my slave so that after preaching to others I myself will not be disqualified." (1 Corinthians 9:27, NIV)The consequences of drawing from his source—letting him fester and entertaining him—are the sacrifice of your very substance and the detriment of your life. Many have come out with grief, crippling guilt, shed tears, and faced mental torment, because these are the outcomes the thief seeks.

He comes only to steal, kill, and destroy, but Christ has come that you may have life and have it in abundance. *"The thief does not come except to steal, and to kill, and to destroy. I have come that they may have life, and that they may have it more abundantly."* (John 10:10, NKJV)Keep the vermin out of your field at all costs and by any means necessary if you desire a good harvest!

The traveler's formula is simple and devastating: **Thought » Desire » Sin » Death.** When sin is fully mature, it births death—spiritual death and eventually physical death. It can mean the death of reputation, marriage, business, or destiny. And greatest of all, it corrupts sexuality—a vital pillar upon which human society stands.

James 1:14–15 (NIV) declares: *"But each person is tempted when they are dragged away by their own evil desire and enticed. Then, after desire has conceived, it gives birth to sin; and sin, when it is full-grown, gives birth to death."*

"For 'Who has known the mind of the LORD so as to instruct Him?' But we have the mind of Christ." (1 Corinthians 2:16, NIV)Take authority over your mind. Do not allow the vermin to contaminate it with filth.

Be careful what you see and hear. If you indeed have the mind of Christ, then make it your intention to manifest it. Understand that evil desires begin with evil thoughts, and when unchallenged, they end in sin—leading inevitably to destruction unless countered.

What must we do? Love the LORD with all our heart, soul, strength, and mind. *"Love the Lord your God with all your heart and with all your soul and with all your mind and with all your strength."* (Mark 12:30, NIV)Replace unholy thoughts with those drawn from the divine source of God. *"Whatever is true, whatever is noble, whatever is right, whatever is pure, whatever is lovely, whatever is admirable—if anything is excellent or praiseworthy—think about such things."* (Philippians 4:8, NIV)

This is a call to reshape your personal environment. You may not be able to change the people around you, but you can replace them with the right company if they continually lead you astray, becoming tools of the traveler against you.

Consecrate yourself by setting boundaries so righteousness can take root. Do not rely on your own understanding, nor on human will alone—it is never enough to destroy the traveler. You need external help. Live by the Spirit so that you do not gratify the desires of the sinful nature. The Holy

Spirit is that external help. He provides the pesticide that keeps the vermin from your field.

How many times have you said or heard, "This is the last time, I promise," or, "I mean it this time"? Are you not tired? Contend for your purity. Fight for it. The Kingdom of Heaven suffers violence, and the violent take it by force. Take what belongs to you by force. *(Matthew 11:12)*

There is a place where God expects you to labor for what you need so that you do not trivialize what He gives—because sweat and tears secure a deeper value. You cannot fall into sin, nor into the new forms of sexual sin in our generation, if you keep in step with Him, die to the flesh, and avoid the pitfalls of temptation.

Walk instead on the path of love, peace, and eternal life, having the mind of Christ that replaces every unholy thought. This mind keeps you alert, thwarting every seeding attempt of the Traveler. This mind makes it impossible to entertain the vermin.

You need not walk in self-condemnation; it was never you alone, but the traveler manipulating the sinful nature within you because of ignorance, weakness, or lack of commitment to sanitize your field with the power of the Holy Spirit. Put to death the sinful nature—the traveler's control mechanism in your life.

"There is therefore now no condemnation to those who are in Christ Jesus, who do not walk according to the flesh, but according to the Spirit." (Romans 8:1, NKJV)Keep in step with the Spirit, and you will never again be a slave to the sinful nature.

Above all, remember: you are never alone. The Spirit of God is always present to lift you up, even when you fall. *"When you pass through the waters, I will be with you; and when you pass through the rivers, they will not sweep over you. When you walk through the fire, you will not be burned; the flames will not set you ablaze."* (Isaiah 43:2, NIV)

So when you rise again and ascend the mountain of God—where true and sustainable purity comes from—the enemy and the floods of immorality will not reach you. Not only because you have subdued and put to death the sinful nature, but because you now live in a higher realm—under the pavilion of the Most High and carried by the Spirit of God. *(Psalms 91)*

"So shall they fear the name of the LORD from the west and His glory from the rising of the sun; When the enemy comes in like a flood, the Spirit of the LORD will lift up a standard against him." (Isaiah 59:19, NKJV) **We are that standard. We must live up to it.**

CHAPTER II
SETTING AND HONOURING BOUNDARIES FOR PURITY

When in battle—contending for your freedom from the enemy who desires you in chains—it would be imprudent to leave your tower without defence, open to attack from whichever direction the enemy may choose to strike. From the very avenues the sinful nature was once fond of, danger arises.

Boundaries must be set to take control of self, for a person without self-control is like a city with broken-down walls, possessing no defence against the attacks of the enemy of your purity. *(Proverbs 25:28).*

Self-control is a byproduct of setting boundaries—first boundaries which you are never to cross, and then boundaries that reflect what you will and will not tolerate from the world outside of you. To cultivate self-control, you must have a clear path of defence against weakness. The answer is found in boundaries.

Persistence is paramount. The righteous man falls down seven times and rises again. *(Proverbs 24:16)* Failures along the way were already accounted for by Grace; it is sin to remain down. Continue to build the walls of righteousness in your life through the discipline of the Word of God, which edifies your inner man.

Buildings and strong fortresses are not built in an instant. It is a journey and a process—with ups and downs—but it inevitably ends in a fortified stronghold of righteousness. You will abound with thankfulness, as Colossians 2:7 teaches: *"Let your roots grow down into him, and let your lives be built on him. Then your faith will grow strong in the truth you were taught, and you will overflow with thankfulness."* (NLT)

Therefore, be careful what you watch and listen to, for your eyes and ears are entrances into your soul. When setting boundaries, the goal is to malnourish the sinful nature—to weaken it and put it to death—not to give it a platform to rise again in power so you revert to its control.

Change the music you hear to positive Christian music. Dispose of anything that triggers you to sin. Consecrate yourself; set yourself apart. Change what you are prone to watching if it contains traces of unrighteousness—nudity, sex scenes, profanity of language.

These measures may seem drastic, but in our current generation, if you truly desire never to crumble again under the influence of the sinful nature, such separation is vital. Of course, this strength is not always immediate; it is grown into.

The more mature you become through the flow of the Word of God in your life, the more capable you become of loosening attachments to worldly pleasures and entertainment—until the sinful nature has nothing left to leverage against you.

The Word of God is eternal. Its principles transcend their context and extend further to build up the Church in every avenue of life. It is pure and established long before you ever existed. Therefore, the divine boundaries He gives—even the personalized ones impressed upon your heart through the conviction of the Holy Spirit—must be honoured, lest the enemy gain a foothold once more and continue to bring you down.

The principles of God have never let anyone down, and they never will. Stay within the boundaries set by the loving Father, and you will reap the fruits of peace, love, and joy—without the sorrow that plagues those who break the hedge set by the Almighty. *"He who digs a pit will fall into it, and whoever breaks through a wall will be bitten by a serpent."* (Ecclesiastes 10:8, NKJV)

With the Word of God written upon the tablets of your heart, you will remain diligent to honour the boundary markers and never violate them, for to do so would be to your own detriment. *"Do not move an ancient boundary stone set up by your ancestors."* (Proverbs 22:28, NIV).

This law transcends territorial boundaries—honour the boundaries, and Peace and Purity shall abound. Your conscience will not be plagued with guilt. Your heart will not grow callous or distant from God. You will flourish in the pastures of purity all the days of your life.

BOUNDARIES FOR SEXUAL-PURITY

UNDERSTANDING SEXUAL-PURITY

"Can a man take fire to his bosom, and his clothes not be burned? Can one walk on hot coals, and his feet not be seared? So is he who goes in to his neighbor's wife; whoever touches her shall not be innocent." (Proverbs 6:27–29, NKJV)

Therefore, a breach of God's boundaries governing sex will end in destruction. Sex is a very powerful part of human function—in fact, it is so powerful that God gave it only within set boundaries, so that it would bring joy and not destruction, fulfillment and not sorrow.

For sexual love, uncontained, can deliver immense destruction into our lives. As Song of Songs 8:6–7 (NIV) declares: *"...for love is as strong as death, its jealousy unyielding as the grave. It burns like blazing fire, like a mighty flame. Many waters cannot quench love; rivers cannot sweep it away. If one were to give all the wealth of one's house for love, it would be utterly scorned."*

When you understand why God created sex and what it is by His original and divine design, you will perceive the importance and gravity of maintaining your sexual purity. If you are not intentional about sexual purity, you can sell your future and sabotage your destiny. Much of your future prosperity—both spiritual and physical—is heavily dependent upon the purity of your sexual stature.

Sexual compromise is the compromise of your future emotional, psychological, and spiritual stability. The violation of pure and holy sexuality, which is one of the three main pillars of human society, is highly detrimental; if it affects society at large, it certainly carries the power to damage your wholeness on an individual level.

God created sex; it was never an accident. The Holy God is the Creator of sexuality—it was created righteous. The temptation to compromise purity is strong in today's world, yet spiritual discipline is vital. God is grieved concerning sex in our generation because humanity, with the influence of the kingdom of darkness, has perverted it.

What was once pure has been tainted with evil. Do not feel guilty about sex; it is a legitimate part of your humanity, nothing to be uncomfortable about in its righteous context.

Sexual perversion will destroy your life. God gave boundaries because when we abuse our sexuality—physically or mentally through sexual immorality—we end up destroying ourselves. We live in a generation where anything sexually appropriate is ridiculed, while everything sexually immoral is celebrated and normalized.

Yet when you remain sexually pure—safe within the pure boundaries of God, not veering off course—you will live in peace. *"The work of righteousness will be peace, and the effect of righteousness, quietness and assurance forever."* (Isaiah 32:17, NKJV)

Sexual sin is overemphasized in Scripture not because it is unforgivable, but because this particular sin causes damage that can at times be irreparable. He who sins sexually sins against his own body. *"Run from sexual sin! No other sin so clearly affects the body as this one does. For sexual immorality is a sin against your own body."* (1 Corinthians 6:18, NLT)

Sexual purity means living morally clean in thought and action, keeping all sexual activity within the confines of marriage or preserving it for marriage. Yet even within marriage, a person can be sexually impure. Even a virgin can possess a perverse sexual mind.

A married person may be filled with lust—an insatiable illness no partner can satisfy—driving them deeper into sin. Pornography has ruined marriages, births adultery, and breeds discontentment, all often rooted in earlier sexual violations. Cleansing through the water of the Word and maturing by the same Word through the help of the Holy Spirit remains the answer.

It is straightforward, true, and exceedingly effective. Should you commit to it seriously, you will see that it is paramount to sexual purity—because true, sustainable purity, the kind that produces satisfaction, wholeness, and contentment, only rises from the higher platform of spiritual maturity in Christ.

You must consciously mark where you are. From there, you will be able to gauge your path, take wise steps, and walk toward growth. Pray as you grow in the Word. Do not be discouraged when you fall; even infants stumble the first time they attempt to walk. It is nothing to be ashamed of—indeed, it is expected.

Rather, keep feeding, keep growing. Sexual purity is not a destination but a permanent lifestyle of intentionality—a renewed mindset—living above the probabilities of backsliding or falling into sexual sin.

THE HIGHER PLANE OF PURITY AND SAFETY

"He who dwells in the secret place of the Most High shall abide under the shadow of the Almighty. I will say of the LORD, 'He is my refuge and my fortress; My God, in Him I will trust.' Surely He shall deliver you from the snare of the fowler and from the perilous pestilence. He shall cover you with His feathers, and under His wings you shall take refuge; His truth shall be your shield and buckler." (Psalm 91:1–4, NKJV)

According to *Psalm 91*, this is the description of the higher plane from which purity rises. When you dwell in the secret place of the Most High, you are kept safe from the pestilence and from every weapon the enemy fashions against your purity. This safety is only possible when a person **abides** in the secret place. The key is precisely that—*to abide.*

As Jesus declared, *"Abide in Me, and I in you. As the branch cannot bear fruit of itself, unless it abides in the vine, neither can you, unless you abide in Me."* (John 15:4, NKJV). Only in God is found that higher spiritual plane upon which purity abounds.

It is there that sexual purity remains shielded and untainted, no matter how high the floods of corruption rise. The ark of your purity will always rise higher. This higher plane must be diligently sought and faithfully remained in; you find it by maturing into it.

Violation of the laws governing sex will hinder your destiny. Breaking any law does not change the law—it only harms the one who violates it. Law exists to govern and protect from lawlessness and anarchy; violating it harms society.

The same is true of God's laws concerning sex. Violating them does not alter what God established—His standards remain true, righteous, and immovable. Rather, the violator destroys himself. As Proverbs 14:12 (NKJV) warns: *"There is a way that seems right to a man, but its end is the way of death."*

There is indeed a way that appears right, yet ends in death. God has already set the righteous sexual way. When you deviate from it, you only cause yourself harm. If the Creator—the One who designed sex—sets the guidelines for its application, and the creation deviates from them, then the creation destroys itself.

"In the way of righteousness there is life; along that path is immortality." (Proverbs 12:28, NIV) Sexual impurity is evil, and it will bring destruction, for sin, when fully matured, produces death.

Concerning the young man seduced into sexual sin by an immoral woman, Scripture gives a solemn depiction of the pits of impurity:

"With persuasive words she led him astray; she seduced him with her smooth talk. All at once he followed her like an ox going to the slaughter, like a deer stepping into a noose till an arrow pierces his liver, like a bird darting into a snare, little knowing it will cost him his life. Now then, my sons, listen to me; pay attention to what I say. Do not let your heart turn to her ways or stray into her paths." (Proverbs 7:21–25, NIV)

Wrong sex is like being led toward slaughter—like a bird caught in a snare. It will cost you your life. It is as an arrow that pierces the liver. Do not let your heart turn to the ways of sexual sin or stray into its paths, for many are the victims who have been brought down by it. The house of sexual sin is a highway to the grave. It begins in pleasure, but it ends in death.

BOUNDARIES FOR SEX: DIVINE SEX-STANDARDS

The first standard is this: **There is a time for sex.** *"There is a time for everything, and a season for every activity under the heavens."* (Ecclesiastes 3:1, NIV).

The phrase *"do not awaken love until it pleases"* appears repeatedly in the *Song of Solomon* (2:7, 3:5, 8:4), where the bride urges the daughters of Jerusalem not to stir up or awaken romantic love before its proper time.

This warning underscores the necessity of patience and restraint in matters of love and intimacy, for sexual love is a powerful and sacred force that must never be prematurely initiated.

God set divine demarcations for sex, establishing that its appointed time is locked within the covenant of marriage—not to be dabbled with outside it. Humanity has suffered destruction for violating this primary law governing sex. Sexual maturity in your flesh does not grant permission for sexual activity outside the boundaries set by God, the Holy Creator of sex.

There is danger in awakening love before it so desires; this love is powerful and unyielding. As Song of Songs 8:6 (NIV) declares: *"...for love is as strong as death, its jealousy unyielding as the grave. It burns like blazing fire, like a mighty flame."*

The second standard is this: **The person you are to do it with can only be one—your spouse, within the covenant of marriage.** God created us to be joined to one of the opposite sex, our spouse. Sexual relations were ordained by God to exist only within a monogamous setting—marriage.

The world has twisted this sacred boundary to such an extent that even people within the church attempt to justify breaking it. Many pretensions arise to coddle the reality that sexual relations outside of marriage are sin.

Yet violation persists: families destroyed by fornicators and adulterers, children born out of wedlock, countless suffering under the wounds of broken homes and absentee fathers. *"Marriage is honorable among all, and the bed undefiled; but fornicators and adulterers God will judge."* (Hebrews 13:4, NKJV).

Multiple sexual partners over the years violate not only God's divine laws but also your own body, your purity, and your vigor. Marriages consummated after such histories often collapse due to comparisons drawn from past experiences—pain God sought to spare us from by giving this law.

Divorce rates skyrocket. Never has there been a generation where marital failure and divorce are so vast and so accepted. This widespread pain and discontent exist because humanity embraced the sinful nature, fueled by the kingdom of darkness, and violated God's laws governing this vital pillar of society.

Concerning marital faithfulness, Proverbs gives a beautiful analogy: *"Drink water from your own cistern, and running water from your own well... Let your fountain be blessed, and rejoice with the wife of your youth."* (Proverbs 5:15–18, NKJV).

The third standard is this: **Sex requires a legal marriage relationship.** Outside of marriage, sex is illegal. Sex outside of marriage is dangerous. Only within marriage is sexual intercourse pure, holy, and undefiled.

Outside it, sex produces pain, heartbreak, societal decay, and divine displeasure. *"The mouth of an immoral woman is a dangerous trap; those who make the LORD angry will fall into it."* (Proverbs 22:14, NLT).

When ancient boundary marks are moved, divine displeasure leaves legal grounds for the enemy to kindle the sinful nature and push a person into sin. *"...and do not give the devil a foothold."* (Ephesians 4:27, NIV). Marriage must be honored by all. It is the springboard of a healthy and functional society under the pillar of sexuality. The Church must be vocal in preserving its sanctity.

Sex is only a blessing **inside** God's boundaries; outside of them, only pain exists. What is kept within its proper standards flourishes and grows in value, but what is violated and made common loses worth. These sexual standards are divine.

Society has lowered them to mediocrity, and the temptation to engage in sexual intercourse outside of marriage has always been great for fallen humanity. Yet this temptation never altered God's laws. Violating God's divine sex standards always leads to disastrous results. Sexual sin always injures someone—individuals, families, businesses, even churches. Sexual desires and activities must be submitted under the Lordship of Christ.

God created sex for procreation, for pleasure, and as an expression of love between a husband and wife. Therefore, sexual experience must remain within marriage to maintain purity, preserve society, and guard morality for future generations. God desires sex to be a joy, a pleasure, and an honorable gift within marriage—not a common and devalued indulgence abused by all. It must be honored. This is true sexual purity.

<u>CONSEQUENCES OF VIOLATING DIVINE SEX-STANDARDS</u>

Just as all sin separates us from God and carries dire consequences for our relationship with Him, so it is with sexual sin. Yet sexual sin carries an additional dimension of destruction: it violates God's divine laws surrounding the pillar of sexuality and destroys the very person who commits it.

"The body, however, is not meant for sexual immorality but for the Lord, and the Lord for the body... Do you not know that your bodies are members of Christ Himself?" (1 Corinthians 6:13–16, NIV) You must therefore keep your body and your entire being sexually pure, for every part of you was redeemed by Christ to live a holy and consecrated life.

Sexual sin hampers your relationship with God. It makes relating to Him increasingly difficult, drawing you further from His presence. Sexual sin, in particular, drains your spiritual strength, floods you with guilt, and burdens you with regret.

"Their deeds do not permit them to return to their God. A spirit of prostitution is in their heart; they do not acknowledge the LORD." (Hosea 5:4, NIV). That "spirit of prostitution" symbolizes the grip of sexual sin; when it is present, it keeps you from acknowledging God and even compels you to make excuses to shelter impurity instead of confronting it.

Sexual sin also hardens the heart and blinds the spiritual eyes. You become obstinate toward God even though He continually extends His gracious hand, compelled by His enduring love: *"All day long I have held out my hands to an obstinate people who walk in ways not good, pursuing their own imaginations"* (Isaiah 65:2, NIV)

Sin blinds the eyes so that one cannot behold nor discern God. *"Blessed are the pure in heart, for they shall see God."* (Matthew 5:8, NIV*). "Without holiness no one will see the Lord."* (Hebrews 12:14, NIV). Impurity creates distance, dullness, and spiritual deafness, shutting the believer out from communion with the Lord.

Yet you are an overcomer. *"I have given you authority to trample on snakes and scorpions and to overcome all the power of the enemy; nothing will harm you."* (Luke 10:19, NIV). You carry divine authority to dismantle every scheme of darkness. Do not allow the weights tied to sexual sin to keep you from your loving Father.

His grace remains sufficient; His forgiveness is already extended. Rise again. Lean upon Him, and through His Holy Spirit He will strengthen you. Take up the Word, mature in Him, and regain your spiritual clarity. The truth remains — He still reaches out His hand for you. Come as you are.

When you persist in sin, the enemy cloaks your eyes and blinds your understanding. *"The god of this age has blinded the minds of unbelievers..."* (2 Corinthians 4:4, NIV.) Access to the Lord becomes hindered, and the heart grows insensitive.

Sexual sin locks the soul away behind hardened walls. *"For the hearts of these people are hardened, and their ears cannot hear, and they have closed their eyes—so their eyes cannot see, and their ears cannot hear, and their hearts cannot understand, and they cannot turn to me and let me heal them."* (Matthew 13:15, NLT). The tragedy of impurity is not only distance from God but the forfeiture of the healing He longs to give.

Sexual sin also leads you to trade destiny for mediocrity. It sabotages your future, your glory, and your victory. Sexual love — powerful and sacred — weakens reasoning when mishandled. *"I am weak with love."* — Song of Solomon 2:5; 5:8 (NLT).

This vulnerability is precisely why God confines sexual love within marriage, where covenantal protection shields it from corruption. The marriage covenant binds husband and wife in exclusive faithfulness, safeguarding this immense force.

For example, in the book of Judges *(chapters 13–16)*, Samson received warnings as clear as daylight concerning Delilah's loyalty to the Philistines — the very enemies seeking his destruction. Each time Delilah attempted to sabotage him, her betrayal was exposed when the Philistines rushed in to capture him.

Yet, blinded by sexual love, Samson returned to her arms again and again. Her manipulation persisted until he revealed his Nazirite secret. Trusting one unworthy of trust, he surrendered the mystery of his strength, and his enemies seized him, gouged out his eyes, and enslaved him.

Pleasure triumphed over destiny. Samson's might could not save him from the consequences of misused intimacy. Though he fulfilled his purpose in a final redemptive act, the cost was catastrophic. His glory was diminished, his freedom forfeited, and the man he once was never returned.

This cautionary tale powerfully reveals the peril of sexual sin. It compromises not only personal purity but the divine destiny placed upon God's children. Just as Samson's strength was tied to his covenantal obedience, our spiritual strength is tied to holiness. When we compromise, we invite the seductive snares that seek to derail our calling, dim our glory, and fracture the future generations entrusted to us.

Sexual sin makes your sex-life sick. Lust is the fruit of a corrupted sexual system — a craving beyond God-given human desire. Lust can never be satisfied; therefore, it renders the soul perpetually discontent.

No spouse can heal this sickness, and no marriage can placate it. Instead, lust wounds the very spouse God gives, poisoning intimacy and eroding trust. Lust is a demon, not a natural desire. What God designed as rightful, holy, marital desire is satiable and finds delight in the spouse ordained by Him.

But lust becomes a demonic stronghold — an evil appetite that grows through the violation of God's sexual laws. When you step outside His boundaries, you awaken cravings that were never meant to exist. What begins small becomes a flood, as appetite grows and entangles the soul in uncontrollable bondage. Even sexual diseases arise in this soil of corruption, testifying to the danger of tampering with God's holy design.

Inevitably, sexual sin distorts your sexual system, rewriting your preferences against God's natural design. Masturbation reconditions the body to find satisfaction in what is sinful, leaving the spouse unable to compete with a fantasy. Pornography engraves scripts into the mind, scripts one later attempts to impose upon their partner — unrealistic, dehumanizing, and dishonoring to the sacred marriage bed.

This forces what is unholy into what God created pure, intimate, tender, and covenantal. When you are sexually sick, marriage begins dying long before you ever enter it. The climax of marital union is sexual intimacy; if the sexual realm is diseased, the very heart of marriage is weakened unto death. You must be whole before you enter marriage, lest you corrupt what God intended to be a fountain of joy and unity.

Sexual lust is a corruption, an intoxication, a demonic amplification of normal human desire. What was once innocent becomes heightened beyond measure, twisted into bondage. Lust inflames the senses, enslaves the will, and perverts what God crafted to be life-giving.

When sex ceases to be a loving, mutual, caring expression within marriage and is instead transformed into a self-serving pursuit of gratification, it no longer serves love — it serves lust. Lust is insatiable, selfish, and devoid of compassion. It dishonors the dignity of another. Love, however, is not lustful.

Scripture declares, *"It does not dishonor others, it is not self-seeking..."* (1 Corinthians 13:5, NIV*)*. When lust is present, it reveals that the love of Christ has yet to be fully formed within the inner man. Maturity in Him is required to purge the corrupting power of lust.

When what is pure is violated, it gives birth to sickly offspring. Sexual diseases emerge, the body withers, and the mind becomes fragmented. Sexual sin damages emotionally, psychologically, and physically.

Solomon, speaking of the man who falls prey to sexual sin, prophesies his end: *"In the end you will groan in anguish when disease consumes your body."* (Proverbs 5:11, NLT.) This groaning is the bitter harvest of impurity — a lifestyle that drains vitality, devastates the soul and destroys the body.

The burden of knowledge is the weight of responsibility that follows it. Now that you know, you must be strong in the Lord and in the power of

His might, (Ephesians 6:10). Steadfastness is not accidental; it is preserved through knowledge and spiritual discipline.

Scripture warns, *"Beware lest you also fall from your own steadfastness being led away with the error of the wicked; but grow in the grace and knowledge of our Lord and Savior Jesus Christ."* (2 Peter 3:17–18, NKJV). You must know the truth to remain anchored in it.

Sexual sin destroys the very fabric of human society, beginning with the individual. Therefore, heed the wisdom of God and embrace

His sexual laws for your preservation. Fortify your spirit in His Word, and you will prevail over temptation. *"My son, pay attention to my wisdom... For the lips of an immoral woman drip honey, and her mouth is smoother than oil; but in the end she is bitter as wormwood, sharp like a two-edged sword. Her feet go down to death, her steps lay hold of hell."* (Proverbs 5:1–5, NKJV.) Sin always begins sweet, smooth, enticing — but its end is bitter, sharp, and deadly.

Sexual sin devalues you and makes you vulnerable to abuse and manipulation. Scripture warns, *"Do not lust after her beauty in your heart, nor let her allure you with her eyelids. For by means of a harlot a man is reduced to a crust of bread; and an adulteress will prey upon his precious life."* (Proverbs 6:25–26, NKJV).

Anything you obtain without cost, regardless of its worth, will begin to lose value in your eyes. When you permit sexual sin into your life, true and pure sexuality becomes devalued. It becomes corrupted, unable to remain in the glorious, untainted form God originally created.

Only through repentance and divine renewal can we be fully restored — but once restored, we must not return to the old ways. When Jesus saved the adulterous woman from her accusers, He did not condemn her; He extended mercy with a commanding charge: *"Go and sin no more."* (John 8:11, NKJV.)

Sexual compromise places you in bondage. *"The evil deeds of the wicked ensnare them; the cords of their sins hold them fast."* (Proverbs 5:22, NIV.) When you engage in sexual sin, you walk into destruction.

Sex never leaves a person unchanged. Within God's boundaries, it enriches and adds life. In violation, it diminishes the soul — and yet still adds something: pain. This pain grows into bondage, where guilt weakens one's resolve, driving the person further into sin and deeper toward spiritual death.

Sexual sin — in every form — is a binding, deadly trap. It ensnares and enslaves the soul. There is no lasting joy for the one living in sexual sin; public laughter turns into private bitterness. Do not allow yourself to be trapped by it — and if you are trapped, free yourself through the truth you encounter in this book.

For *"you shall know the truth, and the truth shall make you free."* (John 8:32, NKJV). Afterward, do the work of God and deliver others from the same snare. *"I discovered that a seductive woman is a trap more bitter than death. Her passion is a snare, and her soft hands are chains. Those who are pleasing to God will escape her, but sinners will be caught in her snare."* (Ecclesiastes 7:26, NLT).

Notice that it is the one who pleases God who escapes her trap. *(Note: This 'woman' symbolizes sexual sin, which makes this relevant to both men and women).* And who pleases God? The one who dwells in the secret place of the Most High, living on the higher plane where purity rises, the realm of spiritual strength born from maturity into Christlikeness. *"LORD, who may dwell in Your sacred tent? Who may live on Your holy mountain? The one whose walk is blameless, who does what is righteous, who speaks the truth from their heart."* (Psalms 15:1–2, NIV.)

Sexual sin renders you defenseless. The apostles, guarding their reputation and the purity of the early church, lived above reproach. Paul testifies, *"We prove ourselves by our purity, our understanding, our patience, our kindness, by the Holy Spirit within us, and by our sincere love."* (2 Corinthians 6:6, NLT)

He continues, *"We use the weapons of righteousness in the right hand for attack and the left hand for defense."* (2 Corinthians 6:7, NLT.) Yet sexual sin — like all sin — strips a person of righteousness. The weapons of righteousness can no longer stand in place to defend you from the enemy's attacks, whether spiritual, reputational, or moral. Sin opens the door to evil spirits, granting them access to tether your life deeper into destructive indulgence.

Righteousness is a self-defending force. It needs no human shield; it defends the saint. The weapons of righteousness protect from slander, malignancy, accusation, and spiritual assault. They uphold and guard a person's reputation. But with sexual sin present, you forfeit this divine defense. You become exposed, spiritually unarmored, and vulnerable — a sitting target for the adversary, having given him a foothold through impurity.

SAFEGUARDS FOR PURE SEXUALITY

Sexuality is immensely important. It is the foundation from which one gains access to another's inner being. *"The two shall become one."* It is the sacred setting from which human society springs. You cannot trivialize or downplay sexuality; it carries the power either to ruin lives or to make them sweet.

Scripture testifies, *"Or do you not know that he who is joined to a harlot is one body with her? For 'the two,' He says, 'shall become one flesh.' But he who is joined to the Lord is one spirit with Him."* (1 Corinthians 6:16–17 NKJV) This is why purity in sexuality is not peripheral—it is foundational to identity, destiny, and divine order.

Sexuality determines and reveals your natural identity—your God-given gender. The Almighty created us male and female, a divinely fixed reality woven into creation itself. This is not merely a biological distinction; it is a sacred design. *(Genesis 1:27)*

And to each—male and female—He assigned roles of great dignity, working together in harmony, all conforming to His loving purpose for mankind and for the flourishing of humanity as a whole.

For each gender, God gave purpose, direction, and position. Yet our fallen world has corrupted these sacred distinctions, birthing destruction, confusion, and conflicts born of resisting God's inerrant principles. Thus, the apostolic charge stands: *"Run from sexual sin! No other sin so clearly affects the body as this one does. For sexual immorality is a sin against your own body."* (1 Corinthians 6:18 NLT)

Sex was present from the very beginning—before the fall—established not as shameful or defiled but as holy, joyful, and divinely ordained. God Himself instituted it for the man and his wife.

As Genesis 1:28 (NKJV) declares: *"Then God blessed them, and God said to them, 'Be fruitful and multiply; fill the earth and subdue it; have dominion over the fish of the sea, over the birds of the air, and over every living thing that moves on the earth.'"* Sexuality was breathed into humanity as part of the original blessing, a conduit through which life, intimacy, unity, and dominion flowed.

When the true value of honoring sexuality as a vital pillar of human society—according to God's standards—is embraced, individuals rise, marriages flourish, and societal healing begins to bloom. Disorder diminishes where purity is restored.

Confusion breaks where truth is honored. Brokenness mends where God's design is upheld. Therefore, every individual must institute prudent safeguards to preserve sexual purity. This is not merely self-protection—it is stewardship of destiny, protection of lineage, and alignment with the divine order through which purity rises from above.

Responsibility as a Safeguard for Purity

Taking responsibility for others—for accountability in this context—keeps you safeguarded by the holy fear of hypocrisy. Leadership by example, leadership forged in purposeful consecration, becomes its own shield. When you carry the weight of influence, the mantle itself fortifies your self-control.

Scripture warns, *"A person without self-control is like a city with broken-down walls."* (Proverbs 25:28 NLT) A leader without restraint becomes exposed, undefended, and susceptible to spiritual collapse.

"But I discipline my body and bring it into subjection, lest, when I have preached to others, I myself should become disqualified." (1 Corinthians 9:27, NKJV)

Therefore, God in His mercy sustains the righteous, placing divine weight around their shoulders so that they may not easily fall. *"Cast your cares on the LORD and He will sustain you; He will never let the righteous be shaken."* (Psalm 55:22 NIV) This sustaining grace often appears in the form of obstacles—divine roadblocks sovereignly set in place to hinder deliberate sin.

Ezekiel echoes this truth: *"If righteous people turn away from their righteous behavior and ignore the obstacles I put in their way, they will die..."* (Ezekiel 3:20 NLT) These obstacles are not hindrances but safeguards—manifestations of the Spirit's conviction urging us back to righteousness.

Ignoring such divine interventions is an act of willful disobedience. The distinction between *willful* and *willing* sin is vital: willful sin is hardened, intentional rebellion; willing sin emerges from weakness or struggle.

To disregard conviction is to desensitize the heart, granting sin territory and allowing the *sarx*—the sinful nature—to regain influence. Thus Scripture warns, *"He who digs a pit will fall into it, and whoever breaks through a wall will be bitten by a serpent."* (Ecclesiastes 10:8 NKJV) Those who ignore God's walls of protection expose themselves to the serpent's bite.

Pride in Your Salvation as a Safeguard

"As for me, may I never boast about anything except the cross of our Lord Jesus Christ. Because of that cross, my interest in this world has been crucified, and the world's interest in me has also died." (Galatians 6:14 NLT) Paul's declaration is a clarion call to every believer: exalt nothing but the finished work of Christ.

When your heart is rooted in the cross, the glitter of worldly pleasure loses its grip. Carnal temptations weaken. The seductions of approval and self-exaltation dissolve. Pride in salvation shifts your identity—no longer driven by earthly appetites, but secured in the triumph of Christ.

This anchoring produces illumination. *"I pray that your hearts will be flooded with light so that you can understand the confident hope He has given to those He called—His holy people who are His rich and glorious inheritance."* (Ephesians 1:18 NLT) When the heart is flooded with light, purity becomes not merely a command but a joy.

The believer stands firmly, remembering that his inheritance is not found in temporary indulgence, but in the eternal glory secured through Christ.

The Love of Christ as a Safeguard

Mutual love—within marriage and among unmarried peers—is a profound safeguard for sexual purity. When relationships are governed by genuine care, Christlike tenderness, and spiritual honor, selfish desires lose power. Lust is displaced by holy affection, and unchecked impulses bow before covenantal love.

Scripture defines this love with precision: *"Love is patient and kind. Love is not jealous or boastful or proud or rude. It does not demand its own way.*

It is not irritable, and it keeps no record of being wronged. It does not rejoice about injustice but rejoices whenever the truth wins out. Love never gives up, never loses faith, is always hopeful, and endures through every circumstance." (1 Corinthians 13:4–7 NLT)

Where this love reigns, purity is preserved. Where this love governs, hearts remain fortified. And where this love abides, sexuality finds its rightful expression—honored, protected, and aligned with God's holy design.

The Divine Love of God

God is love, and love is God; therefore, to mature in God is to mature in love, for God is the very source and embodiment of true love (*1 John 4:8,16*). Everything He does and everything He stands for is an expression of abounding and limitless love toward us. Thus, there is no spiritual maturity—no purity that truly rises from above—if it is not founded upon the eternal foundation of the love of God. Love is the greatest, especially in matters of purity.

Paul unveils the most exquisite portrait of true love in *1 Corinthians 13:4-7*—a portrait that is, in its very nature, the essence of spiritual maturity. He describes a love that moves with patient restraint and gentle kindness, a love emptied of jealousy, free from boastfulness, untainted by pride, and untouched by rudeness.

This love releases the demand to have its own way and is thus self-sacrificing; it refuses to be governed by irritability; it refuses to keep a ledger of offenses. It finds no delight in injustice, yet rejoices fervently when truth prevails. It is a love that holds fast, that refuses to give up, that never relinquishes faith. It is ever-hopeful, enduring with a steadfastness that remains unbroken through every circumstance.

This is the summit of Christian character—the crown of spiritual stature borne by every believer who seeks the higher life in Christ. Such love is not born of fleeting emotions, nor is it sculpted by human resolve. It is the supernatural outflow of knowing Christ deeply and walking in the culture of His Kingdom. It is love shaped by the Spirit, fortified in maturity, and expressed in a life wholly yielded to God.

To bring this truth to its fullness, Paul continues in verse 11: *"When I was a child, I spoke and thought and reasoned as a child. But when I grew up, I put away childish things."* (1 Corinthians 13:11, NLT). Observe how he ties love to maturity: when he was young, this love was not yet fully formed within him. His reasoning was immature, his speech and thoughts ungoverned by the law of love—love that sustains purity, stabilizes character, and anchors the soul.

He then writes in verse 12: *"Now we see things imperfectly, like puzzling reflections in a mirror, but then we will see everything with perfect clarity. All that I know now is partial and incomplete, but then I will know everything completely, just as God now knows me completely."* (1 Corinthians 13:12, NLT). There is a divine knowledge that carries the believer into maturity in God—maturity in divine love, which is God Himself—and from this height flows the elevated spiritual standing from which true purity rises.

Verse 13 seals the matter: *"Three things will last forever—faith, hope, and love—and the greatest of these is love."* (1 Corinthians 13:13, NLT). Therefore, pursue this divine love with diligence. It is indispensable for purity. And the path toward this love is paved through the divine knowledge and experiences gained in the Word of God. More on this maturing in the divine knowledge of Christ Jesus will unfold later in this chapter.

Holy Weakness in Divine Love

When the believer becomes fully matured in the love of God through His Word, a sacred transformation takes place. His divine essence of love begins to move so deeply within you that you become too weak to depart from the path of righteousness. Divine love carries the mysterious power to weaken the resolve of the self-life—dismantling self-sufficiency and drawing you into full dependence upon God, beyond the limits of carnal reasoning.

In the *Song of Solomon*, though speaking of marital love, the Spirit reveals a principle applicable across all dimensions of divine love. The woman cries, *"I am weak with love."* (Song of Solomon 5:8, NLT). Likewise, the Church—the Bride of Christ—is called to be overcome, subdued, and sweetly weakened by His divine love to the point where we no longer live for ourselves but for Him.

As Scripture declares, *"For the love of Christ compels us..."* (2 Corinthians 5:14, NKJV). This compulsion wages war against the self, weakening its stubborn resolve. You become faint—too moved to rebel, too yielded to sin, too overtaken by divine affection to heed the voice of darkness.

May you be **too weak to wander**, too loved to rebel, too conquered by Christ to be conquered by impurity. May the abounding love of God overwhelm you as you mature, causing you to rise into the Purity that comes from Above.

Accountability as a Safeguard for Purity

Accountability stands as a vital safeguard in the pursuit and preservation of purity. When believers commit to honest, transparent fellowship with trusted brethren, they build a spiritual fortress around their lives.

Such relationships form a protective network that guards against temptation and shields the heart from spiritual collapse. Accountability functions as both an alarm and a balm: it exposes hidden struggles, demands honesty, and yet encourages reliance on God's sustaining grace through mutual support. It deters sin by shining light into dark corners, and it nurtures spiritual maturity by reinforcing godly discipline.

Paul's exhortation to the Galatians captures the heart of accountability: *"Carry each other's burdens, and in this way you will fulfill the law of Christ."* (Galatians 6:2 NIV) This charge reveals a profound truth—purity is not an isolated pursuit but a communal pilgrimage.

When we shoulder one another's spiritual challenges, we strengthen each other against the relentless pull of the sinful nature. Accountability becomes the mirror that reveals warning signs early, the voice that calls us back to obedience, and the arm that steadies us when temptation presses inward.

To walk in purity, one must choose accountability intentionally. This means inviting godly voices into your spiritual life—those who will lovingly rebuke when necessary, comfort when wounded, and intercede when weak.

Such intentional connection becomes a wall of defense, making it far harder for the "traveler" of temptation to find lodging in the heart. Accountability transforms isolation into intimacy, vulnerability into strength, and hidden weakness into visible victory. It anchors the believer deeply in the path of righteousness, ensuring that purity is not only pursued but sustained.

"You must warn each other every day, while it is still 'today,' so that none of you will be deceived by sin and hardened against God." (Hebrews 3:13, NLT)

Steadfastness as a Safeguard for Purity

Imagine a sheep conscious of the wolves prowling around it. This holy awareness drives it to stay near the Shepherd, attentive to His voice and wary of straying. With Christ as our Good Shepherd, His voice alone leads us into righteousness, while the enemy whispers lures designed to draw us toward compromise.

The wise believer never walks along the edge of temptation, never toys with the boundaries that define holiness. A single careless step invites danger, for the adversary is patient and predatory.

Scripture warns soberly: *"The devil prowls around like a roaring lion looking for someone to devour."* (1 Peter 5:8 NIV) Such vigilance is not fear but wisdom. Steadfastness in purity, unwavering loyalty to truth, leaves no entry point for the enemy's schemes. This watchful discipline protects the soul from yielding to subtle enticements that often precede greater falls.

Thus the apostle cautions, *"If you think you are standing strong, be careful not to fall."* (1 Corinthians 10:12 NLT) Overconfidence becomes a snare; humility becomes a shield.

Likewise, Peter exhorts, *"Therefore, dear friends, since you have been forewarned, be on your guard so that you may not be carried away by the error of the lawless and fall from your secure position. But grow in the grace and knowledge of our Lord and Savior Jesus Christ."* (2 Peter 3:17–18 NIV) Growth, alertness, and grace form a threefold cord that safeguards purity.

Steadfastness anchors the believer. It demands constant awareness, consistent dependence on the Shepherd's voice, and continual spiritual growth. By God's sustaining grace, steadfast believers remain unswayed, unmoved, and unbroken—walking firmly in purity, guarded by the vigilance that flows from wisdom and the strength that flows from Christ.

Contriteness as a Safeguard for Purity

"Seek the LORD while He may be found; call on Him while He is near. Let the wicked forsake their ways and the unrighteous their thoughts. Let them turn to the Lord, and He will have mercy on them, and to our God, for He will freely pardon." (Isaiah 55:6–7 NIV)

The path of purity begins with repentance—a sincere turning of the whole heart toward God. Contriteness is more than remorse; it is the willing abandonment of sinful ways and corrupt thoughts.

It is the posture of spiritual humility that opens the soul to God's mercy, cleansing, and restoration. Those who bow low in repentance rise high in purity, for contriteness dismantles pride, exposes deception, and repositions the heart beneath the flow of divine pardon.

Isaiah extends this gracious invitation: *"Come, all you who are thirsty, come to the waters; and you who have no money, come, buy and eat! Come, buy wine and milk without money and without cost. Why spend money on what is not bread, and your labor on what does not satisfy? Listen, listen to me, and eat what is good, and you will delight in the richest of fare. Give ear and come to me; listen, that you may live. I will make an everlasting covenant with you, my faithful love promised to David."* (Isaiah 55:1–3 NIV)

Contriteness positions the soul to receive this feast of grace. God calls us away from labor that yields no satisfaction and from sin's empty promises. He invites us to Himself—the only One who satisfies, restores, and sustains.

Jesus echoes this tender summons: *"Come to me, all of you who are weary and carry heavy burdens, and I will give you rest. Take my yoke upon you. Let me teach you, because I am humble and gentle at heart, and you will find rest for your souls."* (Matthew 11:28–29 NLT)

True rest flows from a contrite heart—one that yields to Christ's teaching, bows beneath His yoke, and welcomes His gentle leadership. Contriteness becomes the doorway to renewal, transformation, and purity.

Yet Scripture warns of the peril of resisting conviction, for "the wages of sin is death." *(Romans 6:23)* And the writer of Hebrews delivers a sobering warning: *"Dear friends, if we deliberately continue sinning after we have received knowledge of the truth, there is no longer any sacrifice that will cover these sins."* (Hebrews 10:26 NLT)

Conviction becomes essential—a holy pain that pulls the heart away from destruction and into life. Paul reflects on this in his rebuke to the Corinthian church:

"I am not sorry that I sent that severe letter to you, though I was sorry at first, for I know it was painful to you for a little while. Now I am glad I sent it, not because it hurt you, but because the pain caused you to repent and change your ways. It was the kind of sorrow God wants his people to have, so you were not harmed by us in any way. For the kind of sorrow God wants us to experience leads us away from sin and results in salvation. There's no regret

for that kind of sorrow. But worldly sorrow, which lacks repentance, results in spiritual death." (2 Corinthians 7:8–10 NLT)

Godly sorrow produces repentance—a sorrow born of conviction that draws the soul to Christ. Worldly sorrow only produces despair, shame, and death. Paul then lists the fruits of true repentance:

"Just see what this godly sorrow produced in you! Such earnestness, such concern to clear yourselves, such indignation, such alarm, such longing to see me, such zeal, and such a readiness to punish wrong. You showed that you have done everything necessary to make things right." (2 Corinthians 7:11 NLT)

This is the power of true contrition—it awakens zeal, purges compromise, and restores righteousness. Yet worldly sorrow binds the mind with six chains that strangle purity:

The Six Cords of Mental Bondage:

• **Self-doubt:** Anchor your identity in Christ; knowing you belong to Him slays doubt.

• **Self-pity:** Trust God's strength; His presence breaks the cycle of inward despair.

• **Self-despise:** Remember your worth—purchased at the price of Christ's own blood.

• **Guilt:** Embrace God's forgiveness and forgive yourself; guilt loses its grip.

• **Regret:** Release the past by accepting God's mercy and extending forgiveness.

• **Denial:** Face truth with humility; let God's light expose and dismantle darkness.

Breaking these cords frees the conscience, heals the mind, and restores spiritual clarity. Contriteness—humble repentance, godly sorrow, and brokenness before the Lord—is foundational to true purity. It births freedom, fortifies holiness, and positions the believer to walk triumphantly in the light of God's mercy.

TYPES OF BOUNDARIES

"Do not move an ancient boundary stone set up by your ancestors." (Proverbs 22:28, NIV)

Boundaries—especially those established by God through His Word—exist for our protection, preservation, and flourishing. When we move or ignore these "ancient boundaries," whether moral standards or spiritual precepts, we invite unnecessary trouble into our lives.

God knows the human tendency toward gradual compromise; the smallest, seemingly harmless step away from His ways can eventually lead us into deep spiritual peril.

Proverbs 22:14 (NLT) reinforces this warning: *"The mouth of an immoral woman is a dangerous trap; those who make the LORD angry will fall into it."* The erosion of God's protective covering often begins with small acts of willful disobedience. These subtle increments—often justified, overlooked, or dismissed—are never unnoticed by God.

They slowly corrode the divine protection and favor we once possessed. In this vulnerable state, the enemy strategically prepares traps, exploiting our willfulness and pride. Moving outside God's established boundaries is ultimately a decision to walk outside of His covering.

This principle is echoed again in Proverbs 24:12 (NLT): *"Don't excuse yourself by saying, 'Look, we didn't know.' For God understands all hearts, and He sees you. He who guards your soul knows you knew. He will repay all people as their actions deserve."*

Once you have received knowledge of God's standards, you also bear the weight of responsibility to uphold them. Shifting boundaries—ignoring your personal, relational, or protective safeguards—places your spiritual well-being in direct danger.

Types of Boundaries:

• **Personal boundaries**

• **Relationship boundaries**

• **Protective boundaries**

Each of these serves as a divine marker—reminding you to honor God's order, respect what has been established, and protect your heart from the slow encroachment of sin. Living within God's boundaries is not about restriction; it is about abiding in the security, strength, and blessing of a life truly set apart.

PERSONAL BOUNDARIES

Personal boundaries define what you will and will not tolerate in your life. They serve as protective limits that preserve your spiritual integrity and guard against compromise.

Paul urgently instructs in Ephesians 4:17–19 (NLT): *"With the Lord's authority I say this: Live no longer as the Gentiles do, for they are hopelessly confused. Their minds are full of darkness; they wander far from the life God gives because they have closed their minds and hardened their hearts against him. They have no sense of shame. They live for lustful pleasure and eagerly practice every kind of impurity."*

We do not set personal boundaries from pride or scorn for those in the world. Rather, boundaries are acts of love for Christ and acts of self-preservation in the divine purity granted through His Spirit.

Paul's resolve to remain disciplined expresses this truth: *"I discipline my body and bring it into subjection, lest, when I have preached to others, I myself should be disqualified."* (1 Corinthians 9:27 NKJV)

Allowing others—friends or peers who promote immorality or revel in sinful talk—to encroach upon your limits erodes your purity. Bad company corrupts good morals. *(1 Corinthians 15:33)* The call is clear: do not live as they do; firmly set and uphold personal boundaries to defend your purity and spiritual growth.

Ephesians 5:1–13 (NIV) exhorts believers to imitate God with lives marked by love and holiness:

"Follow God's example, therefore, as dearly loved children and walk in the way of love, just as Christ loved us and gave himself up for us as a fragrant offering and sacrifice to God. But among you there must not be even a hint of sexual immorality, or of any kind of impurity, or of greed, because these are improper for God's holy people. Nor should there be obscenity, foolish talk or coarse joking, which are out of place, but rather thanksgiving... For you were once darkness, but now you are light in the Lord. Live as children of

light… Have nothing to do with the fruitless deeds of darkness, but rather expose them."

In today's world, corrupted by media and a social culture intoxicated with sinful nature, setting boundaries is urgent. Exposure to obscene stories, coarse jokes, and sexualized media rekindles sinful desires. This incremental contamination creeps back in when entertained, eroding spiritual defenses.

Therefore, clear guidelines in all relationships are essential. Feed your spirit with purity—meditating on what is true and lovely—to starve the sinful nature, which must be put to death. When lax, complacency increases, making spiritual failure more likely. Stay anchored by disciplined prayer, and never forget to feed and nourish your spirit with the Word of God for spiritual growth and strength.

The apostle Paul warns strongly against wrong peers: *"Do not be yoked together with unbelievers. For what do righteousness and wickedness have in common? Or what fellowship can light have with darkness? What harmony is there between Christ and Belial? Or what does a believer have in common with an unbeliever?… For we are the temple of the living God."* (2 Corinthians 6:14–16 NIV)

God commands, *"Therefore, come out from them and be separate, says the Lord. Touch no unclean thing, and I will receive you."* (2 Corinthians 6:17 NIV) Those around you either strengthen your purity or pull you into compromise. Our environment profoundly affects our spiritual condition.

Paul's fervent exhortation to cleanse ourselves from everything that defiles body and spirit speaks directly here: *"Because of these promises, dear friends, let us purify ourselves from everything that contaminates body and spirit, perfecting holiness out of reverence for God."* (2 Corinthians 7:1 NLT)

Therefore, shield yourself with the purity that comes from maturing in Christ through the Word of God and the influence of the Spirit of God. *"Cling to your faith in Christ, and keep your conscience clear. For some people have deliberately violated their consciences; as a result, their faith has been shipwrecked."* (1 Timothy 1:19 NLT)

Entertainment today is a key tool the enemy uses to violate the conscience in order to draw believers away from spiritual disciplines and allow the sinful nature to rise again, ultimately shipwrecking their faith.

Today, marketing and entertainment have become heavily sexualized—designed to corrupt young minds and desensitize society to immorality. This flood of sexual impurity contaminates innocence and distorts God's holy design for sexuality.

Unchecked Entertainment Feeds the Sinful Nature

We live in a world obsessed with healthy eating habits—good foods and bad foods, clean diets and junk food. There is an entire culture built around fitness, discipline, physical health, and wellness, yet very few ever pause to recognize that the same principles govern the spiritual life.

"Physical training is good, but training for godliness is much better, promising benefits in this life and in the life to come." (1 Timothy 4:8 NLT) Paul shows us that the spirit also requires a healthy lifestyle and a disciplined "diet."

Just as someone committed to physical fitness may allow a small "cheat day" snack yet refuses to abuse it for fear of derailing progress, many choose absolute discipline—no cheat days at all—so they may attain and maintain their goals. Likewise, within the inner man there is healthy food and junk food. The Word of God is the nourishment that builds and fortifies your spirit, while entertainment functions like snacks—small, permissible pleasures when kept in proper measure.

"You say, 'I am allowed to do anything'—but not everything is good for you. You say, 'I am allowed to do anything'—but not everything is beneficial." (1 Corinthians 10:23 NLT) Entertainment in itself is not sinful; the danger emerges when it is unregulated—when it becomes your primary intake, replacing the Word of God as the anchor of your life.

Just as a fitness enthusiast knows that consistent workouts and clean eating are made useless when matched by equal indulgence in junk food, so too does spiritual progress collapse when one overindulges in entertainment.

Mindless entertainment—endless scrolling on social media, constant surfing online—exposes the heart to a stream of images and ideas that subtly feed the sinful nature. For those once captive to lust or still fighting its pull, the internet is full of triggers capable of dragging you back into old patterns, undermining your consecration and sabotaging your pursuit of freedom. When entertainment ceases to be a small, regulated treat after diligence and becomes "soul food"—overprioritized, unbounded, and consumed without discipline—you empower the sinful nature and weaken your spiritual resolve.

In such a condition, you undo the impact of feasting on the Word of God by continually nourishing the soul—the very place where the sinful nature resides—with worldly content, which, as established, is its primary diet. Therefore, do not be deceived: poor habits and unchecked indulgence inevitably lead to sin.

Man is an Incremental Creature

Movies with nudity—even a little—are a gateway to greater sin. They are still a portion of pornography. We are creatures of increment; the sinful nature exploits this design by slowly conditioning us. We were created by God to be creatures of increment. With God, the little taste we get of His goodness only awakens us to seek more of Him.

But on the flip side, this same incremental nature is how our conscience becomes seared in the place of illicit pleasures. The first time we do something wrong, we are overwhelmed with guilt—we are broken, deeply sorry, and we repent.

The second time we do it, we still feel guilty, but not to the same degree as before. That is already an increment. The third time, then the fourth time, guilt weakens, tolerance grows, and eventually we begin making excuses for it, which inevitably leads into bondage to sin.

That is why Scripture warns against resetting ancient boundaries. These are not merely physical land markers—they include personal, moral, and spiritual boundaries. The more you cross them, the more you shift them, until eventually the boundaries are no longer what they used to be, nor what they were meant to be.

So with such movies, a small capacity is built within you. Later on, a film with slightly more nudity or more detailed sex scenes no longer feels like a leap. Before long, it is no longer enough; you end up in pornography, which leads to masturbation, fornication, and all the like. All of this stems from the one time you allowed yourself to abuse your personal boundaries, thinking it an innocent dabbling. We are incremental creatures.

Hence the biblical warning: moving ancient boundaries—physical or moral—ignites divine displeasure and spiritual danger. Small transgressions build capacity for greater sin. This slippery slope leads from minor compromises to the full spectrum of sexual sin: pornography, masturbation, fornication, and more. *"Whoever breaks through a wall will be bitten by a serpent."* (Ecclesiastes 10:8 NKJV) When you set that boundary line, you must never cross it, nor allow anyone else to cross it.

Because of this, you are the one to blame when you fall into sexual sin. It never begins with the sin itself—there is always a gradual decline in moral boundaries. Increment upon increment eventually ripens into full-blown sin because you tolerated what you were not supposed to tolerate.

And sin, when fully mature, gives birth to death. Your spiritual life faces spiritual death, your relationship with God is negatively affected, and for some people, it never recovers from that blow—where the mind becomes fully seared against the conviction of the Holy Spirit.

Knowing you are an incremental creature should shape every decision. No matter how strong-willed you believe yourself to be, human nature will override it if you allow your God-ordained boundaries to shift.

Understanding that you are an incremental creature should govern your decisions. It does not matter how strong you think you are—if you allow someone to move your ancient boundaries, as Scripture forbids, then as a creature of increment, it will not be the last time you compromise.

"I am a sinner if I rebuild the old system of law I already tore down." (Galatians 2:18 NLT) After transformation, breaching new boundaries places you back into sin. Even subtle boundary crossings can rekindle old

sins if left unaddressed. For instance, once bound by pornography and later committed to purity, watching *any* nudity can restart a dangerous pattern.

"We take captive every thought to make it obedient to Christ." (2 Corinthians 10:5 NIV) *"My old self has been crucified with Christ. It is no longer I who live, but Christ lives in me."* (Galatians 2:20 NLT)

Breaching boundaries attempts to resurrect what died at salvation. You will reap consequences if you indulge thoughts that agitate your conscience—your personalized boundaries safeguard your holiness.

As an incremental creature, a small capacity is formed, and it will naturally grow unless you notice it and deal with it immediately. It is so subtle that you think nothing of it, but it is the first step in a chain of increments. As Paul explains: *"Everything is permissible—but not everything is beneficial. Everything is permissible—but not everything is constructive."* (1 Corinthians 10:23 NIV)

Turn away from worthless things: *"Turn my eyes away from worthless things; preserve my life according to your word."* (Psalm 119:37 NIV)

Compromise is not always blatant sin; recognizing this truth protects your spiritual fervour. Subtle compromises—the small indulgences, the minor curiosities, the "it's not really sin" moments—often open unseen doors.

Such moments may permit distracting spirits, the "traveler," to slip into your life. If something excites you carnally, tempts you, lingers in your mind, or agitates your focus, then it is wrong for you to indulge in. Seek the face of God instead.

Paul reinforces this reality when he teaches that if you indulge in something your conscience is not comfortable with, *then to you it is sin.* He writes,

"But if you have doubts about whether or not you should eat something, you are sinning if you go ahead and do it. For you are not following your convictions. If you do anything you believe is not right, you are sinning." (Romans 14:23 NLT)

This reveals the sacredness of personalized boundaries—God-tailored limits meant to safeguard your purity. Violating your conscience violates your purity. 'Everything is permissible, but not everything is beneficial'. If it weakens your conscience, stirs temptation, or dims your spiritual clarity, it becomes sin *to you*. Therefore, turn your life from worthless things—those subtle distractions that carry no eternal value and quietly drain spiritual strength.

Compromises are not restricted to what is openly known as sin. Understanding this truth will preserve your spiritual fervour. Many believers fall not through obvious iniquity, but through small permissions—minor entertainments, subtle indulgences, and quiet neglects that accumulate over time. These seemingly harmless allowances open gates for the "traveler" —a distracting spirit—to influence, weaken, and derail. Guard your gates. Guard your mind. Guard your boundaries.

Pharaoh's hardened heart is a sobering illustration of incremental resistance. The narrative unfolds in **Exodus chapters 7–14**. God began with smaller signs through Moses—signs Pharaoh's magicians could imitate. Emboldened by this slight sense of power, Pharaoh hardened his heart.

The next time, the increment of defiance had already begun. Plague after plague, his heart hardened in proportion to the increasing severity of God's judgments. Finally, the death of his firstborn broke him, and he released Israel. Yet even then, as a creature of increment, he reverted back to defiance and pursued them.

This repeated pattern—this ingrained habit—carried him to a great loss, for the Egyptian armies perished as the waters of the Red Sea collapsed upon them after Israel crossed safely on dry ground. This is the frightening extent of human incremental nature: it can lead a man all the way to his own ruin.

God created man as a creature of increment—with reasoning, capable of growth, innovation, and advancement—called to dominion *(Genesis 1:28)*. This design is pure, holy, and purposeful. But without vigilance, that same incremental nature becomes a downward spiral into compromise and destruction.

The more we taste of God's love, the deeper our hunger for Him should grow. His incremental design is meant to protect us, not destroy us—to draw us upward into holiness, not downward into sin. When anchored in God, increment becomes consecration; when untethered from God, increment becomes corruption.

RELATIONSHIP BOUNDARIES

Relationship boundaries protect you from the world and from others. Refuse to be in any relationship where there is any form of domestic abuse—physical, verbal, or mental. Unlike an infant, once you are old enough to understand, you are partially responsible for how you are treated because you choose what you will tolerate. Unpopular as it may be, this truth stands: God calls us to stand firm and not be doormats to the world.

For example, if your spouse continually mistreats you, you share responsibility because you allow it. The more you accept it, the more it escalates—*for man is a creature of increment.* What starts small grows worse over time.

If you are with someone who, in anger, appears likely to become physically abusive—even if they have not yet—you must end the relationship immediately. This illustrates why relationship boundaries are so vital; abuse always begins subtly, and early assertion protects you from greater harm.

Because of this, you are responsible when you fall into sexual sins. It never begins with the sin itself, but with a gradual decline in moral boundaries—increment upon increment—that ripens into full-blown sin because you tolerated what you should not have.

Sin, when fully mature, brings death—including spiritual death where your conscience becomes seared against the Holy Spirit's conviction. For a great marriage, take responsibility not only for your behavior toward your spouse but also for the behavior you accept from them. *(More on this in the next chapter)*

PROTECTIVE BOUNDARIES

Protective boundaries nurture and safeguard the relationships closest to you. They extend your personal boundaries to shield your marriage and your children. In today's corrupt generation, it is paramount to raise children in the way they should go—so they do not stray from that path. *"Train up a child in the way he should go, and when he is old he will not depart from it."* (Proverbs 22:6 NKJV)

These boundaries are non-negotiable in every Christian household and must never be broken—even at the risk of offending those outside who seek to intrude. The price is too great to risk their innocence being corrupted by the world before parents have had the chance to properly guide and educate them.

Protective boundaries dictate when you must cut someone off. *"Bear one another's burdens, and so fulfill the law of Christ."* (Galatians 6:2 NKJV) Yet Scripture also says, *"For each one shall bear his own load."* (Galatians 6:5 NKJV)

The "burden" in verse 2 refers to a heavy weight, meaning we should help others in times of deep need. In verse 5, the burden refers to personal responsibility. Everyone must bear their own responsibilities and choices.

If someone refuses, you have biblical grounds to separate: *"For even when we were with you, we commanded you this: If anyone will not work, neither shall he eat."* (2 Thessalonians 3:10 NKJV)

Protective boundaries help you discern when to support and when to separate in love, guarding your household's purity and spiritual health.

THE SINFUL NATURE'S SET PATTERN OF CONTROL OVER YOUR LIFE

It is always the same—nothing new under the sun. The tactic never changes. Notice the pattern and break loose. The cycle of sin begins with temptation. Then, you place your trust in yourself, believing you are strong enough to withstand it. Such naivety immediately seals your fate, as it did Samson's. Then you inevitably fall into sin. Next comes guilt, which weakens you to the point where you no longer have the strength to fight the same temptation again.

Conviction strengthens you; guilt weakens you. After that, you enter the loop—always the same pattern. Soon your heart becomes insensitive and callous. What was once unthinkable becomes as swift as an afterthought because man is a creature of increment.

When you trust yourself, you place confidence in the flesh—and thus, you will fall. *"Cursed is the man who trusts in man and makes flesh his strength, whose heart departs from the LORD."* (Jeremiah 17:5, NKJV)

When you put self-trust in the face of temptation, you have already lost the battle. Instead, trust in the Spirit, for the Word says: *"For we are the circumcision, who worship God in the Spirit, rejoice in Christ Jesus, and have no confidence in the flesh."* (Philippians 3:3 NKJV)

Mark the pattern well: **Temptation → Self-trust → Sin → Guilt → Temptation...** The cycle is predictable. The escape is supernatural. It is found in the Word of God.

THE FOLLY OF SELF-TRUST

"How foolish can you be? After starting your new lives in the Spirit, why are you now trying to become perfect by your own human effort? Have you experienced so much for nothing? Surely it was not in vain, was it?" (Galatians 3:3-4, NLT)

As we have already seen, man is an incremental creature. Yet man is also weak. The sinful nature has been present in humanity since the fall from Eden. Since then, man's incremental drive—meant to explore, grow, and expand—has been perverted, especially in the realm of sin.

"When a crime is not punished quickly, people feel it is safe to do wrong." (Ecclesiastes 8:11 NLT) This reveals the incremental nature of humanity.

However, freedom from the law of sin and death comes by accepting Christ. The Holy Spirit enters our lives as a deposit guaranteeing the greatness to come. But it does not end there; you must stand strong and grow strong in the Spirit. Temptations will come.

Once you were lost in sexual sin; now you have tasted freedom. Yet Jesus taught that when an evil spirit is driven out, it later returns to see if its former dwelling is still vacant. If it finds the house empty, it summons seven spirits more wicked than itself, making the final condition worse than the first. (Referenced in **Matthew 12:43–45; Luke 11:24–26.**)

What was once a sin you repented deeply over becomes abundant—even reinforced by demonic influence—until your conscience is seared and you begin to defend it. This happens when you trust yourself instead of the Holy Spirit, neglecting spiritual disciplines like prayer, devotional reading, and hearing God's Word.

If you take these things for granted, forgetting the ongoing spiritual war between light and darkness, you open yourself to the enemy's attack. But when you remain vigilant, disciplined, and growing, the Holy Spirit increases His presence in you. When evil spirits and temptations return to test you, they find their former home now occupied by the strongest and holiest Spirit—Christ Himself—and they flee.

This is the way of the prudent. After growing strong in the Spirit through God's grace and shedding the sin that entangles, do not grow complacent. You are safer on the higher plane of spiritual existence—the secret place of the Most High—where you abide in Christ, dwell deep in the Holy Spirit, and walk in spiritual maturity.

To remain righteous, live not by human strength but by faith: *"Behold the proud, his soul is not upright in him; But the just shall live by his faith."* (Habakkuk 2:4 NKJV)

GROWING IN THE KNOWLEDGE OF THE WORD OF GOD FOR PURITY: BECOMING CHRIST-LIKE

Growing in the knowledge of the Word of God for purity is the journey of becoming Christ-like—a progressive ascent into maturity in Christ and the glory to be attained. Paul declares in Philippians 3:8–16 (NKJV):

"Yet indeed I also count all things loss for <u>the excellence of the knowledge of Christ Jesus my Lord,</u> for whom I have suffered the loss of all things, and count them as rubbish, that I may gain Christ; and be found in Him, not having my own righteousness, which is from the law, but that which is through faith in Christ, the righteousness which is from God by faith; <u>that I may know Him</u> and the power of His resurrection, and the fellowship of His sufferings, being conformed to His death, if, by any means, I may

attain to the resurrection from the dead. Not that I have already attained, or am already perfected; but I press on, that I may lay hold of that for which Christ Jesus has also laid hold of me. Brethren, I do not count myself to have apprehended; but one thing I do, forgetting those things which are behind and reaching forward to those things which are ahead, I press toward the goal for the prize of the upward call of God in Christ Jesus. Therefore let us, as many as are mature, have this mind; and if in anything you think otherwise, God will reveal even this to you. Nevertheless, to the degree that we have already attained, let us walk by the same rule, let us be of the same mind."

In these verses, three main pillars emerge: **the excellence of the knowledge of Christ**, **the desire to know Him deeply**, and **the upward call of God in Christ Jesus**. Identity and purpose—true, pure, and unshakable—are discovered in the depths of knowing Christ. This knowledge is not limited to reading and application; it is the Spirit-driven shaping of your life over seasons, a lifestyle of continuous pursuit.

Spiritual maturity is less about reaching a final destination and more about relentless pressing forward—forgetting what lies behind and reaching toward what is ahead. Every intentional step deepens transformation into Christlikeness.

This journey demands discipline, grace-fueled growth, the shedding of hindrances, and the courage to keep ascending despite challenges. It is the wholehearted embrace of the upward call to live in holiness, purity, and the power Christ provides.

STARTING FROM THE BOTTOM UP: THE UPWARD CALL OF GOD

There are three callings in the Kingdom of God:

1. **Christian Calling** – where God calls you into salvation.

2. **Vocational Calling** – calling into service or ministry: Apostles, Pastors, Politicians—your divine assignment.

3. **The Upward Call** – the call into perfection; maturity in Christ.

Paul already understood the first two. The Upward Call is distinctive—it is the holy summons into spiritual perfection, into the fullness of maturity. According to Paul, this is the *one thing* we must strive for.

This call is universal to all believers: a deep hunger for the depths of Christlikeness, counting everything else as loss compared to the surpassing excellence of knowing Christ. It is the focusing of mind, body, and spirit on one pursuit: Christ in all His fullness, who alone can fill your life.

THAT I MAY KNOW HIM

Philippians 3:10 – *"that I may know Him and the power of His resurrection, and the fellowship of His sufferings, being conformed to His death."*

How could Paul—an Apostle, church planter among the Gentiles, a man who encountered the risen Christ, who spent three years in the desert of Arabia in primal consecration (*Galatians 1:17–18*), who received revelation directly from the Lord Jesus (*Galatians 1:12*), and whose conversion itself was a supernatural encounter (*Acts 9*)—still confess that he needed to know Christ more?

Dear reader, this is the sobering reality: even at Paul's height of maturity, the knowledge of Christ remains an endless ascent. We search fervently through prayer, Scripture, and communion with the Holy Spirit—seeking fresh revelation, divine encounters, and deeper understanding.

We are creatures of increment, but God is limitless in perfection and glory. For this reason, we never cease growing. We continue to mature, to be built up in the Spirit, and to rise "Above."

The higher we ascend, the more we become like Him. The more He increases, the more we decrease. *(John 3:30)* As the remnants of the carnal, sinful nature die off, His holy life fills us—through maturity, through purity, through transformation. This is the journey of becoming Christ-like: rising from carnality to maturity, from maturity to glory, until Christ is formed in us.

Going back to Philippians 3:10, the word *"know"* carries layered meaning within the Greek language. The first level is **Gnosis**—general knowledge that comes through information. This is where we all begin as readers of the Word of God.

Here, the appetite for Scripture awakens, and we start growing on the spiritual milk of the Word. *(1 Peter 2:2)* Over time, this knowledge matures into solid revelation, becoming evident in application within our daily lives. That development ushers us into the second level.

The second level is **Aido**—to perceive, to know through the senses; sensory knowledge through what we have seen, heard, or touched. At this stage, the Word of God begins to take living root in us. We not only know what Scripture says—we begin to live it.

We gain life experiences through its truths, standing firmly on the faith it imparts. Here, our spirits grow stronger, and the sinful nature begins to lose its grip at the helm of our lives. It is dislodged because we are maturing in the solid food of the Word. Visible manifestations of God's truth begin to show in our lives. With this grounding established, we advance into the third level of knowledge.

The third level is **Tsunesis**—intelligence, comprehension, understanding. It is the moment when the information you first received in Gnosis, and lived through in Aido, becomes illuminated with deeper insight. Through diligent reading, meditation, and the quickening work of the Holy Spirit, you return to Scripture and see new dimensions.

What once seemed obscure now becomes obvious. You have matured—advanced in the knowledge of the Word of God. Remaining in this level over the various seasons of life prepares the ground for the fourth level.

The fourth level is **Epistemone**—experiential knowledge. This is the place of standing firm in truth because you have lived it and proven it. You not only know the Word, you have tested it, and it has never failed you. Across time, through battles and victories, the Word becomes an anchor.

David himself speaks from this level when he declares: *"I have been young, and now am old; yet I have not seen the righteous forsaken, nor his descendants begging bread."* (Psalms 37:25, NKJV). David's conviction was born from a lifetime of witnessing God's provision—even during exile, warfare, and persecution.

It echoed the revelation first given to Abraham, who named God *"Yahweh Yireh"*—*"Jehovah Jireh"*—in *Genesis 22:14*. This is **Epistemone**—where the Word becomes tangible, undeniable, lived reality.

Beyond this is the fifth and highest level: **Ginosko**, leading into **Epignosis**—full discernment, superior knowledge, intimate knowing. This is the deep, experiential oneness described as the intimacy between husband and wife. It is this knowledge Paul speaks of in *Philippians 3:10*.

It is the excellence of the knowledge of Christ—a depth that births spiritual maturity and Christlikeness. This goes beyond awareness and beyond comprehension; it is relational knowing, heart to heart, spirit to Spirit. To mature in Christ, you must journey toward this intimacy, yearning within your inner man to experience it. Feast fervently on the Word until your spirit matures enough to touch this depth. This is the *Purity that Rises from Above—Maturity in Christ.*

The knowing Paul refers to is a lifelong career—you will never outgrow it. You may access deep revelations along the way, but this knowledge will always remain an intimate pursuit, a holy obsession. Make this your sacred ambition: to know Him as He knows you.

This intimate knowledge of Christ is birthed through three realms:

- **The power of His resurrection**

- **The fellowship of His sufferings**

- **Being conformed to His death**

These experiences arise as we journey toward the place of becoming. Every prerequisite, every stretch, and every season of maturation in Christ opens the doorway to deeper intimacy with Him. For *"the glory of this latter temple shall be greater than the former"* (Haggai 2:9, NKJV). Therefore, you must rise—rise *Above* your current level in the knowledge of Christ, ascending into the fullness of who He is.

THE POWER OF HIS RESURRECTION

The power of the resurrection is the foundation of walking in the new life in Christ Jesus. It is the reality of crucifying the misdeeds of the sinful nature through the strength granted by the Holy Spirit as you mature in the excellence of your knowledge of Christ Jesus. *"I have been crucified with Christ; it is no longer I who live, but Christ lives in me; and the life which I now live in the flesh I live by faith in the Son of God, who loved me and gave Himself for me."* (Galatians 2:20, NKJV)

Now you live by faith, not by the power of the self-life. This is what Paul means by "know Him." Your life is no longer animated by ambition, personal gain, or loss—it is Christ alone. For those who reach this dimension, *"To live is Christ, and to die is gain."* (Philippians 1:21, NKJV)

When these three realities converge—the power of His resurrection, the fellowship of His sufferings, and being conformed to His death—you enter into a deep and transformative knowledge of Christ. This is the **excellence of the knowledge of Jesus Christ our Lord**.

"Yet indeed I also count all things loss for the excellence of the knowledge of Christ Jesus my Lord, for whom I have suffered the loss of all things, and count them as rubbish, that I may gain Christ." (Philippians 3:8) With this excellent knowledge, you gain Christ Himself. You receive all the virtues transmitted through these dimensions.

The name **Jesus** means *Salvation*. You begin to experience the salvation of the Messiah in every dimension of life—even in the valleys, even through trials. Whatever the circumstance, you uniquely encounter His saving power.

The name **Christ** means *the Anointed One*. In this realm, you begin to walk in the anointing of the Holy Spirit without measure. This anointing is the final requisite in the journey toward maturity in Christ, empowering you to wield the authority necessary for your highest impact in life. This is the place God desires for you—the highest plane of maturity, where the sinful nature loses its grip, where you are truly free, bound only by Christ Himself and the upward call of God through Him.

Then comes **Lordship**. He releases the virtues of His Lordship upon you. You walk in authority because He is Christ Jesus, *our Lord*. Maturing into Him grants you the grace to steward salvation for those you are called to, to carry the anointing with integrity in the place of divine appointment, the love of Christ, and to walk in the authority that overflows from God's power.

BEING FOUND IN HIM

Then you are found in Him—your identity, a **SON OF GOD**. *"And be found in Him, not having my own righteousness, which is from the law, but that which is through faith in Christ, the righteousness which is from God by faith."* (Philippians 3:9)

This is the essence of sonship: knowing it as identity, not as title; knowing God as Father—not as a role, but as identity. This is the final place of *becoming*—the realm of knowing Christ and attaining maturity in Him.

Here, spiritual growth reaches its fullness, and identity becomes rooted—not in performance, law, or self-righteousness, but in the righteousness that comes by faith. Paul affirms this maturity with clarity:

"Let all who are spiritually mature agree on these things. If you disagree on some point, I believe God will make it plain to you. But we must hold on to the progress we have already made." (Philippians 3:15–16, NLT) This is the inheritance of those who rise—those who press toward the upward call, those who become.

FORSAKING THE SINFUL NATURE AND EMBRACING GROWTH THROUGH THE WORD

Now that you know the importance and essence of the journey to true purity lies only through the Word of God, embrace growth through the Word and enjoy the process. As you mature, the Holy Spirit is there for you. *"God is our refuge and strength, a very present help in trouble."* (Psalm 46:1, NKJV)

To attain the glory of Maturity in Christ—the Purity that rises from above—there is only one thing standing in your way: the life of the 'self,' the sinful nature. To attain Maturity in Christ, founded in the love of Him in and through you to the world, is to be selfless, for Love *"… is not self-seeking."* (1 Corinthians 13:5, NIV)

This selflessness opposes the sinful nature, which is only self-serving. It must be forsaken and put to death, making way for the life of Christ in you to thrive. You must embrace growth through the Word of God to do this. Isaiah 55:7–9 exhorts the sinner:

"Let the wicked forsake their ways and the unrighteous their thoughts. Let them turn to the Lord, and he will have mercy on them, and to our God, for he will freely pardon. "For my thoughts are not your thoughts, neither are your ways my ways," declares the LORD. "As the heavens are higher than

the earth, so are my ways higher than your ways and my thoughts than your thoughts." (Isaiah 55:7–9, NIV)

The words of verses 8–9 are God's message to those serving the sinful nature—not to the saints under the New Testament. According to Paul, *"Who has known the mind of the LORD that he may instruct Him? But we have the mind of Christ."* (1 Corinthians 2:16, NKJV)

As believers mature, we think God's thoughts, do His will, and live for Him—our minds and thoughts built upon His Word. Writing is thinking in action; it reveals the author's mind. Likewise, the written Word of God is God's thoughts—His teachings, His precepts, His plans for you to have a future and hope.

When we read and internalize Scripture and see it by the revelation granted by the Holy Spirit received at salvation, we bear the thoughts of God—from the mind of Christ.

Therefore, we repent where we have breached boundaries and let incremental habits lead us into sin—where the sinful nature ensnared us through successive boundary breaches, particularly through sexual sin. Joel 2:13 calls us to repentance: *rend your heart, and not your garments; Return to the LORD your God, for He is gracious and merciful, slow to anger, and of great kindness; And He relents from doing harm."* (Joel 2:13, NKJV)

This is a call to repentance through a contrite heart, which is not only a safeguard for purity but also a heart God cannot reject. *"The sacrifices of God are a broken spirit, A broken and a contrite heart—These, O God, You will not despise."* (Psalm 51:17, NKJV)

When we read, hear, and internalize the Word of God, it builds our inner being. Speaking of the fivefold ministries—prophets, apostles, pastors, evangelists, and teachers—Paul says God equips the saints for ministry through these graces and edifies the body of Christ:

"For the equipping of the saints for the work of ministry, for the edifying of the body of Christ." (Ephesians 4:12, NKJV) The Greek word for *edify* here is **Oikodomeo**, meaning literally to build a house or structure. Without this building process, we are vulnerable—left baseless and structurally weak—open to the enemy's attacks, even those arising from the sinful nature within us as temptation tempts.

Only a spiritual structure strengthened by the Word of God can resist and become a stronghold, weaponizing righteousness to overcome the devil and his dark schemes.

Cleansed, Renewed, and Made New

"As far as the east is from the west, so far has He removed our transgressions from us." (Psalm 103:12, NKJV) This vivid distance signifies the complete and irreversible removal of our sins when we come to Him. It affirms that there is no turning back; the past is cleansed, and we stand declared righteous.

In the midst of life's weariness and burdens, Jesus' tender invitation beckons: *"Come to Me, all you who are weary and burdened, and I will give you rest."* (Matthew 11:28, NIV) This rest is not mere physical relief but profound spiritual renewal—a refuge where worn souls find peace and strength to continue the journey of sanctification.

God confronts us with a holy challenge in Isaiah 1:18: *"'Come now, let us settle the matter,' says the LORD. 'Though your sins are like scarlet, they shall be as white as snow; though they are red like crimson, they shall be like wool.'"* (Isaiah 1:18, NIV) This promise reflects the transformative power available through repentance and God's grace—our sins, however deep and stained, can be wholly cleansed.

Paul encapsulates this dynamic renewal: *"Therefore, if anyone is in Christ, he is a new creation; old things have passed away; behold, all things have become new."* (2 Corinthians 5:17, NKJV) This new creation experience breaks the chains of past failures and sets the believer on the pathway to lasting holiness and victory over sin.

Though sin's sting and the law's power remain formidable— *"The sting of death is sin, and the power of sin is the law."* (1 Corinthians 15:56, NIV)—our hope resounds in God's triumph: *"But thanks be to God! He gives us the victory through our Lord Jesus Christ."* (1 Corinthians 15:57, NIV)

Hence, for those who abide in Christ and walk in His righteousness, the apostolic declaration is sure and comforting: *"There is therefore now no condemnation to those who are in Christ Jesus, who do not walk according to the flesh, but according to the Spirit."* (Romans 8:1, NKJV)

With these truths etched in your heart, the journey toward purity intensifies. The foundation is set—the past forgiven, rest found in Christ, and newness embraced. From this place of spiritual wholeness and victory, we now turn to the crucial context of purity in marriage, where these principles continue to find practical and profound application—indeed, even more profoundly.

The next chapter will illuminate this sacred covenant, guiding you to build a pure and God-glorifying union.

CHAPTER III
PURITY IN MARRIAGE: GROWING CLOSER TO GOD

The marriage covenant is patterned after the covenant between Christ and His Bride—the Church. Therefore, every obligation a husband has toward his wife must be patterned after the purity of Christ in His obligation to the Church, His Bride. Likewise, every obligation a wife has toward her husband must reflect the purity required of the Church as she fulfills her devotion to her Groom, Christ Jesus our Lord.

Marriage was given to humanity by God before the fall of man in the Garden of Eden. It was, and remains, God's perfect will for mankind—even before sin ever entered our awareness. Sexual intercourse was designed by God and ordained pure; however, it must remain within the boundaries of marriage as God established it.

"Marriage is honorable among all, and the bed undefiled; but fornicators and adulterers God will judge." (Hebrews 13:4, NKJV). The Greek word

translated "bed" here is (**"koitos,"**), literally meaning sexual intercourse. Therefore, according to the Bible, sexual intercourse within marriage is pure, holy, and should be honored by all. As it is written, *"Therefore a man shall leave his father and mother and be joined to his wife, and they shall become one flesh."* (Genesis 2:24, NKJV).

The very first recorded words spoken by a human in Scripture are a love poem from the man to his wife. *"Then the rib which the LORD God had taken from man He made into a woman, and He brought her to the man. And Adam said: 'This is now bone of my bones and flesh of my flesh; She shall be called Woman, because she was taken out of Man.'"* (Genesis 2:22–23, NKJV).

Adam expressed awe and relief that one of his own kind had been brought to him—a companion suitable and intimately connected. From the beginning, sexual and intimate love between a man and his wife was established as pure. God gave it as His perfect gift for humanity, intended for marriage and for fulfilling His command to be fruitful, multiply, and subdue the earth.

The basic purpose of marriage is fourfold: **love, companionship, pleasure, and procreation.** From this foundation, God established the springboard for all human society. His perfect vision for marriage also includes this profound truth: marriage typifies the depths of worship between man and the Spirit of God—a sacred union in which man fulfills his purpose before his Creator.

"Give unto the LORD the glory due to His name; Worship the LORD in the beauty of holiness." (Psalm 29:2, NKJV). In giving humanity the gift of sexual union, God also provided a physical type to help us grasp the spiritual depths of worship.

Thus, marriage becomes a platform that elevates our understanding of the excellent knowledge of Christ. It is a place where love matures and experiential knowledge grows, mirroring the intimate union God seeks with those who worship Him in spirit and in truth.

The climax of marriage is the sexual climax—a physical type of the spiritual climax between the human spirit and the Spirit of God in worship. Sexual union in marriage becomes a divine "looking-glass," a holy lens through which we glimpse the depth of our relationship with God.

It becomes a portal of understanding regarding the divine nature of intimacy with Him. Marriage is pure and holy; sex is God's perfect design and will for your life—but always within His ordained boundaries.

Just as worship belongs to God alone, sexual intimacy belongs to your one spouse alone. It must be preserved for them only, just as your worship is preserved for God alone. There are no "road-tests," no trial runs to gain practice or experience. As instinctively as a newborn knows to nurse at its mother's breast, and as naturally as humanity would fall to its knees should God manifest His glory, so too is the divine instinct of marital intimacy.

You will know what to do, and you will experience the purest, most intimate pleasure ordained by God as a reward for marital covenant. Therefore, do not succumb to the deceptions of the world leading you toward sexual compromise. Purity is a gift—one to be preserved for your spouse within the lifelong commitment of fidelity in marriage.

PERVERSIONS OF PURE SEXUALITY: DEPARTING FROM GOD'S HEART

But after the fall of man, everything was corrupted. Sexual union—gate-kept for marriage only—was part of that equation as well. We fell in every aspect from God's perfect design.

Though God's redemption plan through Christ Jesus gives us the platform to rise back up, finally reconciled to the Father and begin the journey to maturity in Christ (*Colossians 1:21–23*), we must still, throughout our lives, ensure that we preserve the purity of sexuality by God's design.

We must guard it from the infiltrating corruption of the world that seeks to influence it with impurity—even within our marital union.

Because of the fall of man from the Garden of Eden, sexual perversion became a cancer to human society. Many ills sprung from it as Satan worked to distort our view of sexuality because it meant so much to God.

Being a platform that typifies God's perfect union with His people through their worship-based relationship with Him, the mission to corrupt it meant shutting a key avenue for man to grow in understanding spiritual intimacy with the one true God. This was a bid to disconnect humanity from the very source of our true life indeed—God Himself.

If you corrupt sex, you distort man's perfect view of God's perfection. Heartbreaks, rape, adultery, fornication—these were never God's will, but the filth-children of sexual perversion. This distortion changed the purpose of sex in human society into a selfish tool for self-gratification. Thus pornography, orgies, and all other unnatural sexual practices arose to further deviate from God's perfect image of sex.

Satan went all out to ensure man would never find his way back to God's perfect design. His goal was to deviate us from the source, where we could truly gain a natural understanding of the heart of God. Sex in marriage is essential for growing in the understanding of our relationship with God.

These deviations immediately impact that truth and destroy us. The more morality decays, the more sin evolves. Today, there is such a thing as virtual sex through masturbation and sex toys—further cancelling God's will and divine intention for purity in sexuality.

The sinful nature thrives in discovering that the perfect pleasure God locked within a perfect union can be accessed cheaply and devalued. Humanity has been demoralized. Everything is sexualized.

The pure waters God created exclusively for marriage now spill into our faces—from screens, billboards, product advertisements, music videos, strip clubs, and wild parties where multitudes gather for atrocious sexual sin. The lust of the flesh has grown insatiable and perverted. Sin has evolved.

People now invent new ways to sin sexually—all to keep the marriage bed impure. We live in a world where anything sexually pure is considered unpopular and foolish. Virginity has been painted as a sin, and losing it early is praised. Many brag about it. We have lost our perception of purity.

The deeper humanity sinks into sexual sin, the more the lines of purity and the path to righteousness in God are marred. Being creatures of increment, every new experience of sexual sin—every new gratification—gives birth to more lustful desire.

This creates an insatiable hunger for more. Many have tried different things, birthing new evils. Pornography has levels and layers, and its lightest forms are fed to children and teenagers through movies. The increment grows until it ends in unrealistic abominations designed to pervert the human mind from appreciating what true and pure sex is—so that even within marriage it remains perverted.

Same-sex attraction is a product of the insatiable lust born of sexual deviation. Growing discontent with the natural order, this lust spread to those of the same sex, now further evolving into newer forms. Marriage was ordained by God for man and woman only.

Now the world has crafted its own deviations—the world we live in today has clearly fallen far from God's perfect design. Concerning these things, it is written in Romans 1:24–28 that God gave them up to a depraved mind because of their hardened hearts:

"Therefore God gave them over in the sinful desires of their hearts to sexual impurity for the degrading of their bodies with one another... Because of this, God gave them over to shameful lusts. Even their women exchanged natural sexual relations for unnatural ones. In the same way the men also abandoned natural relations with women and were inflamed with lust for one another. Men committed shameful acts with other men, and received in themselves the due penalty for their error. Furthermore, just as they did not think it worthwhile to retain the knowledge of God, so God gave them over to a depraved mind, so that they do what ought not to be done." (NIV)

Human society has been deeply marred from God's perfect purity. This is Satan's calculated plan to drive man further and further away from the heart of a loving God. The further he pushes humanity from God, the better for him. Corrupting our knowledge and perception of sexuality—a crucial pillar of human society—is his greatest tactic.

When sexuality is corrupted, the entire perception of natural order becomes unclear. The lines between right and wrong blur. Sexuality is the springboard of all humanity; from it we draw our natural identities—our genders.

God created them male and female; there is no other gender. It is a binary reality: *"So God created mankind in His own image, in the image of God he created them; male and female He created them."* (Genesis 1:27, NIV).

Therefore, when sexuality—the pillar through which humanity derives natural identity—is corrupted, future generations born under its blurry view carry the confusion further. They grow into unholy morphs of what God created. This is where gender confusion was born: boys thinking they are, or can become, girls and vice-versa.

Some even suggest that gender exists beyond the binary reality God established. This is all the work of Satan, described in *Revelation 12:9* as the ancient serpent who leads the whole world astray. He is not only the "accuser of the brethren" (*Revelation 12:10*) after leading humanity into sin, but also the 'confuser' of the brethren, for he is a liar and the father of lies (*John 8:44*).

All the confusion in the world today stems from Satan's lies. This is especially true regarding the explosion of sexual perversion unlike anything humanity has seen. The marriage bed has been dishonored.

Many no longer believe in the beauty and perfection of the marriage covenant. This loss of faith in God's perfect design draws us away from His heart, painting an image of God as 'imperfect' in our eyes.

Families are destroyed. Divorce tears at the fabric of God's perfect covenant as corruption creeps into marriages through worldly influence. Pain, dissension, unfaithfulness, and domestic violence are all products of impurity in the pillar of sexuality.

They break the covenant between couples. Such pain plagues humanity because of the perversion of God's perfect design. All sexual sin derails humanity; born from the lust of the sinful nature, it evolves through incremental appetite, and the generations born in this order further catalyze it.

"The wrath of God is being revealed from heaven against all the godlessness and wickedness of people, who suppress the truth by their wickedness, since what may be known about God is plain to them, because God has made it plain to them. For since the creation of the world God's invisible qualities—his eternal power and divine nature—have been clearly seen, being understood from what has been made, so that people are without excuse." (Romans 1:18–20, NIV)

GENERATIONAL MORAL DECAY

Because of this moral decadence saturating the world, the influence upon the younger generations—and those yet to arise—is devastating. They inherit not the purity of God's design but the corruption of the age into which they are born, assuming it to be appropriate and normal.

Thus, the strength of youth, once intended to be directed toward productive work, divine assignment, and the purposes of God, is siphoned away by sexual immorality. The vigor meant for destiny is wasted on sin.

Young girls now lust with insatiable desire for the ungodly and the unrealistic, shaped by the fallen world and its immoral, sexually driven content—fueled through the internet, peers, entertainment, and even corrupted family environments.

As a result, they become defiled and abused by lustful men and women of this fallen world, driven relentlessly by a sinful nature (*Ezekiel 23:1–21*). It is a calculated trap—a satanic design—to destroy future generations before they even begin to blossom.

Young men too lose their lustre, their strength, and their vitality long before age can naturally diminish them. They waste away in the beds of immorality, sinning against their own bodies through masturbation and destroying their own posterity.

Pulled by the moral decay of the world, they trade destiny for indulgence, virtue for vanity, and divine potential for destruction. They enter adulthood hollow—carrying wounds, dysfunctions, and regrets that could have been avoided—thus producing a bitter society, broken because the pillar of pure sexuality was perverted.

But nobody finds joy or true happiness in these pits. Do not be deceived. They are trapped, and inwardly they groan, longing for escape—yearning unknowingly for holiness, for restoration, for truth.

Their souls ache for the manifestation of the true sons and daughters of God, those who carry the light of righteousness. *"For the creation waits in eager expectation for the children of God to be revealed."* (Romans 8:19, NIV).

Therefore, the Church bears the burden of restoration—to rectify the wrongs of a fallen culture and to shine a path of return to purity. We are the lamp set upon the hill, the standard raised for a deceived generation, calling them back to righteousness, back to salvation, back to the maturity of Christ—the upward call of God.

"Let your light shine before others, that they may see your good deeds and glorify your Father in heaven." (Matthew 5:16, NIV).

This is why the apostolic warning of Scripture must resound again in our day:

1 Corinthians 6:9–11 (NKJV) *"Do you not know that the unrighteous will not inherit the kingdom of God? Do not be deceived. Neither fornicators, nor idolaters, nor adulterers, nor homosexuals, nor sodomites, nor thieves, nor covetous, nor drunkards, nor revilers, nor extortioners will inherit the kingdom of God. And such were some of you. But you were washed, but you were sanctified, but you were justified in the name of the Lord Jesus and by the Spirit of our God."*

Here lies the truth: corruption is not the final destiny of humanity. In Christ, the fallen can rise; the impure can be washed; the broken can be restored; the deceived can be awakened; and the sexually perverted can be purified by the Spirit of our God. This is the hope for generations yet living and generations yet unborn.

THE SIN OF ADULTERY

Pornography in marriage is mental adultery. It is a sexual sin. *"You have put pagan symbols on your doorposts and behind your doors. You have left me and climbed into bed with these detestable gods. You have committed yourselves to them. You love to look at their naked bodies."* (Isaiah 57:8, NLT)

Though spoken in spiritual terms to describe the people's idolatry, God reveals through the prophet Isaiah a truth that applies even physically. As we have established, the spiritual and the natural are interlinked.

Notice the symbols. In our world today, anyone may keep these "images" hidden in a folder on their phones—viewing them in secret—drawing further away from intimacy with their spouse. In doing so, they commit themselves to "climb in bed," even mentally, with these other people. They begin to love the image of their naked bodies and, in so doing, breed discontent within their marriage.

Pornography breaks marriages. There are countless systems in this world—strategically constructed by the kingdom of darkness—to ensure that marriage never succeeds. Why?

Because the fallen human mind loses its closest and most perfect chance at a "looking-glass" into the knowledge of God. If marriage were honored by God's standard—even among unbelievers—they would still come to the Church when marriage time came.

And the Church, entrusted with the covenant, would declare the gospel truth. For marriage itself typifies the covenant of salvation. People may come for what they think is merely a physical union, yet by hearing the truth of God's design, they would be confronted with the depths of God and be saved.

A corruption of marriage is a corruption of man's divine looking-glass into the holy realm of God. Marriage is not meant to be officiated by governments issuing cheap contracts lacking spiritual substance. It must be officiated by those entrusted with its guardianship. The Church must restore the truth: **marriage is a covenant, not a contract.**

A contract is built on mutual distrust, designed to protect two people from each other's potential unfaithfulness, imposing penalties for breaking its terms. But a covenant is built on mutual trust. It is the foundation of every marital relationship—trust that your spouse will keep the vows made on the wedding day. This covenantal trust teaches us the deeper knowledge of faith in God, whose promises never fail.

Adultery, therefore, is a great sin against the marital covenant because it introduces infidelity, even in the mind. It remains sinful even if both partners choose to watch pornography together. That is simply allowing the world to pollute the marriage bed and open a portal to demonic activity. It is unacceptable.

Pornography is sexual sin, and in marriage, it is mental adultery. Each spouse becomes inflamed with their own vain imaginations and lusts toward strangers. When satisfaction should be found in one's spouse alone, comparisons arise—and such is evil incarnate, bringing corruption into the marriage covenant.

Adultery Typifies Idolatry; *"You have committed adultery on every high mountain. There you have worshiped idols and have been unfaithful to me."* (Isaiah 57:7, NLT)

As adultery breaks the perfect covenant union between a man and his wife, so it typifies the breaking of our covenant union with God when we give ourselves to the idols of life.

Marriage is an exclusive relationship in which man and woman become one; adultery tears apart this God-ordained unity. When people turn from God and give their love to idols, He calls it spiritual adultery.

Sexual union—created to typify the divine for our carnal understanding—has been so perverted by evil that it has become an idol in itself. *(Romans 1:24-25)* Something meant to reveal God has become something worshiped by fallen humanity.

Such corruption cries out for restoration. Idolatry pulls us away from God's heart and from under His covering of righteousness, leaving us vulnerable to greater ungodliness. Then sins like adultery abound, and the marriage covenant is weakened throughout society.

As sexual climax typifies the depth of worship when the human spirit meets the Spirit of God, so adultery—even when only imagined—is the typification of idolatry before God. Jesus taught this clearly:

"But I tell you that anyone who looks at a woman lustfully has already committed adultery with her in his heart." (Matthew 5:28, NIV)You are called to belong to your spouse alone—with all your being—for the two have become one.

"The husband should fulfill his wife's sexual needs, and the wife should fulfill her husband's needs. The wife gives authority over her body to her husband, and the husband gives authority over his body to his wife. Do not deprive each other of sexual relations, unless you both agree to refrain from sexual

intimacy for a limited time so you can give yourselves more completely to prayer. Afterward, you should come together again so that Satan won't be able to tempt you because of your lack of self-control." (1 Corinthians 7:3–5, NLT)

THE LOOKING-GLASS OF DIVINE PERFECTION: CONVICTIONS ABOUT SEXUAL PRACTICES

The sweetness of sexual intimacy is man's most profound learning platform for grasping the deeper realities of his covenant union with God—realities the human mind cannot naturally comprehend.

Sexual intercourse, that is, the union of the female and male sex organs, is what God designed to create this experience, ushering man and woman into a realm of understanding through the sacred mystery of sexual climax.

No other sexual practice brings the same experience or typifies what God intends for us to perceive. For that reason, every other sexual practice—even within marriage—that isn't the straightforward and natural order God created is simply a product man's explorative desires.

We may coddle such practices as exploratory or innocent, and perhaps some are. Some can be considered intimate foreplay; yet more often than not, we allow the influence of the world's sexual perversions to creep into the marriage bed, causing defilement, pain, discomfort, and emotional turmoil.

The real question must be asked: *"Is this pure, mutual practice, and intimate exploration of one another's bodies, or is this practice conceived from the corrupt nature of the world?"* Nothing born out of the world's corruption should ever be introduced into God's perfect union.

God does not wish to strip you of pleasure—far from it. In marriage, He expects you to enjoy sexual pleasure to its fullness, for He designed you to crave this kind of fulfillment through sex alone.

This design preserves purity of mind and unity of heart, ensuring that both spouses fulfill one another, rather than fostering one-sided pleasure and selfish gratification. Sex was created to serve **both**, for it was made **for both**.

Let no perversion created by the fallen world creep into the marriage bed. Such intrusions corrupt God's perfect covenant union and bring unnecessary pain and destruction.

There are lust-driven sexual practices that are harmful to the physical body and can only be referred to as sexual abuse; yet marriage is a covenant of love and care. Why then place your spouse in a position of discomfort, harm, abuse, or emotional upheaval? A covenant calls for protection, not exploitation.

Above all, be led by the conviction of the Holy Spirit upon your conscience. When He governs your inner witness, you cannot entertain the devil's deviations from divine design—even unknowingly.

For Scripture teaches, *"everything that does not come from faith is sin."* (Romans 14:23, NIV). Paul makes it clear that to act against your faith-informed conscience is sin. Likewise, Romans 14:14 (NIV) declares: *"If anyone regards something as unclean, then for that person it is unclean."* And *1 Corinthians 8:12* warns that leading someone to violate their conscience is a sin against Christ Himself.

Therefore, as you guard the marriage bed from the perversions of the world, you must likewise guard the integrity of your own conscience and that of your spouse in your intimate explorations. Do not lead one another into practices that violate conviction, for in so doing, you invite sin and jeopardize your good name.

Your sexual life is to remain private, just as the marriage bed resides behind closed doors; this boundary preserves purity from corruption and confusion. Yet sexual purity according to the teachings of God's Word must be public, vocal, and boldly upheld—especially among the young. Their foundation must be laid early so they do not depart from righteousness as they mature. *"Train up a child in the way he should go, and when he is old he will not depart from it."* (Proverbs 22:6, NKJV).

THE NEED FOR RIGHTEOUS REFORMS

During the days of Ezra and Nehemiah, who were governors of Judah in their respective periods (*Ezra* 7–10; *Nehemiah* 1–13), sexual immorality afflicted God's people—the returned exiles. Yet God desired a restoration, one that included rebuilding the temple and the city walls of Jerusalem, to bring His people back to Himself in His perfect design so they could flourish once more as His worshippers.

For change to occur within the community, God first ordained Ezra and later Nehemiah to carry out righteous reformations of the people's practices—to rebuke, correct, and restore them so that righteousness could flourish again.

Because of the reformative work of these men, the identity of God's people began to shine anew, and their faith and worship were restored and set in motion. This restoration would not have been possible without these reforms, for sexual sin—like all sin—distances us from God, and therefore it needed to be eradicated.

As it was then, and as the example is given to us in the Word of God by those who went before us, so must it be today. The Church must rise up in strength, purity, and righteous indignation to correct this terrible wrong—*the perversion of purity and sexuality*. It is for this reason that the Apostle Paul began his work of correction and righteous reforms by giving the **Instructions for Marriage** in the seventh chapter of his first letter to the Corinthian church:

"But because there is so much sexual immorality, each man should have his own wife, and each woman should have her own husband." (1 Corinthians 7:2, NLT).

Marriage is God's design and solution to manage human sexual desires righteously. God created these desires, but He also created the time, place, and covenant of marriage for them to be fulfilled in the purity of His design—as a looking-glass into His perfect oneness with His beloved people. Marriage provides a committed and holy context for sexual relations, preventing the destructive consequences of sexual immorality outside of that covenant.

Because the world continues to infiltrate our lives with sexual immorality, Paul advises believers to retreat into God's perfect covenant of marriage: *"But if they can't control themselves, they should go ahead and marry. It's better to marry than to burn with lust."* (1 Corinthians 7:9, NLT).

Though not the highest motivation for marriage, in a generation drowning in moral decadence, it becomes vital for preserving sexual purity. Marriage provides a platform for the pure expression of sexual desire. Yet it is advisable to first find sexual wholeness in regard to purity before entering marriage—more on this later in the chapter.

Sexual temptations are difficult to withstand because they appeal to the natural desires God created within us, and this becomes especially challenging for those who have not yet matured in spiritual strength to steer their lives away from the control of the sinful nature. Marriage provides God's way to satisfy these natural desires and strengthen both partners against temptation.

This is why it is a vital addition on the journey to the higher plane of spiritual stature, where true and sustainable purity rises from. Married couples have the responsibility to care for one another:

"The husband should fulfill his wife's sexual needs, and the wife should fulfill her husband's needs. The wife gives authority over her body to her husband and the husband gives authority over his body to the wife." (1 Corinthians 7:3–4, NLT). Therefore, husbands and wives should not withhold themselves sexually, but should fulfill one another's needs and desires.

This is God's perfect will—a pure platform for the expression of sexual desire and sexual pleasure, a holy place for the saints to retreat from the evil temptations of sexual sin outside God's will.

"Do not deprive each other of sexual relations, unless you both agree to refrain from sexual intimacy for a limited time so you can give yourselves more completely to prayer. Afterward, you should come together again so that Satan won't be able to tempt you because of your lack of self-control." (1 Corinthians 7:5, NLT).

The Church must therefore be faithful to teach purity and preserve the integrity of sexuality as a pillar of human society. The solution lies in prioritizing spiritual growth to overcome temptation, through a stature built on the edifying and strengthening Word of God.

The Church must teach and work to rectify the pollution that has plagued marital unions in our generation, both physically and spiritually, through the power and authority granted to it by Christ through the Holy Spirit. More on this rectification will unfold later in this chapter.

CONCLUSION

Paul teaches in *1 Corinthians* chapter 7 primarily to restore divine order and to ward off misconceptions regarding marriage within the church community. His aim is to safeguard purity within the marriage covenant. Marriage serves as a clear and vivid picture of God's relationship with us.

It is God's best natural means to explain, in a tangible and understandable way, the depths of His union and knowledge of us—a spiritual intimacy so deep the human mind cannot fully comprehend it.

Yet the marriage covenant symbolizes this relationship, with sex within marriage typifying the depths of our true worship of Him. This sacredness is so pure that any impurity marring it would drastically affect and distort how human society perceives God.

Throughout Scripture, God consistently uses physical means to typify spiritual truths, enabling humanity to grasp them. For instance, God used the clay in the hand of the potter as a powerful symbol for His people.

He sent the prophet Jeremiah to a potter's house with clear instructions to use the imagery and actions witnessed there to convey the message of the LORD to His people—a vivid declaration of His sovereign shaping of their destiny (*Jeremiah 18*).

This is why the marriage covenant must be kept from corruption by the toxic influence of the world set to compromise it, for it is our only looking glass to understand the depths of our relationship with Christ—the Bridegroom of the Church—side by side.

The heights of corruption and sexual sin in the world have become severe, all in Satan's agenda to destroy man by distorting his perfect view of God and how to relate to Him. Thus, the marriage covenant must be protected with drastic measures—for the sake of all humanity.

It cannot be infiltrated, polluted, or mocked by the world's perversions of it. By corrupting sexuality, God's "classroom" teaching platform—the very system ordained to help humanity understand Him more—is twisted and dismantled.

As a result, each new generation sees a distorted version of marriage and, by extension, an imperfect and unloving God. Marriage has been made to look broken, flawed, and disposable. This falsehood has become the "truth" many now embrace.

Jesus addressed this danger of distorted perspective when He taught: *"The eye is the lamp of the body. If your eyes are healthy, your whole body will be full of light. But if your eyes are unhealthy, your whole body will be full of darkness. If then the light within you is darkness, how great is that darkness!"* (Matthew 6:22–23, NIV).

His words illustrate the catastrophe of false perception—the eye representing perspective, the light representing truth, the darkness representing falsehood, and the body representing the mind. In essence, Jesus warns: if what you believe is light is actually darkness, then the deception is profound.

If the Church continues to shrink back from teaching purity concerning this vital pillar of human society, future generations will live under the shadow of this darkness—believing lies about marriage to be truth. Humanity will continue drifting away from understanding and cherishing the purity of God's covenant with us, which He freely offers to all who accept faith in Christ into their lives.

Divorce rates and adultery have skyrocketed—even within the Church—because the warrior spirit of the Church sleeps and refuses to rise against the encroaching darkness. Even same-sex marriages have further twisted the pure design of marriage in our generation, now being condoned by those who call themselves 'church' but are in truth the false church.

The true Church of Christ must protect the purity of marriage, for marriage reveals who we are to God, who He is to us, and who we are in Him. It is a divine looking glass into the beauty of His holiness—a seeing-portal into His divine nature. We cannot afford to lose its clarity. We cannot allow its perfect image to be blurred.

And yet, there is still hope. The LORD still calls His people to rise. We must heed that call and shine our light in this dark world: *"Arise, shine, for your light has come, and the glory of the LORD rises upon you. See, darkness covers the earth and thick darkness is over the peoples, but the LORD rises upon you and His glory appears over you. Nations will come to your light, and kings to the brightness of your dawn."* (Isaiah 60:1–3, NIV).

CORRECTING THE PERFECT DESIGN OF PURITY IN MARRIAGE: RESTORING TRUTH AND BALANCE

INTRODUCTION

In the journey to right the wrongs, we must build appropriate foundations based on the truth of the Word of God. Marriage was created pure by God and stands as the perfect heterosexual and monogamous union between a man and a woman—typifying the spiritual relationship between Christ and the Church, that is, God and mankind.

This is the perfect design God instituted and advocates for in His pure and inerrant Word, captured across the pages of Holy Scripture.

Purity in marriage, therefore, is the adherence to God's perfect design, upheld by the purity attained through spiritual maturity in Christ. As both husband and wife grow into Christlikeness—answering the upward call—they gain the strength and wisdom to function in marriage as God intended.

For Christ's spiritual union with His Bride is a perfect covenantal fellowship where purity abounds and conflict dissolves, for all are attuned to one another in God Himself.

It is important to understand that marriage is an office—one that demands spiritual maturity. It is not a covenant to waltz into carried by limerence or emotional impulse. It is a holy, lifelong partnership ordained by God to display the glory of His perfect union with His people (*Psalm 29:2*).

Though Paul counsels in *1 Corinthians 7:9* that it is better to marry than to burn with lust, sexual pressure is not the best motive for marriage. This is why marriage is for the spiritually mature to wield. With maturity comes the strength to overcome sexual sin long before marriage, and the capacity to cultivate steadfast love—love that endures all things.

With this maturity, one gains the strength and integrity necessary to choose the right marriage partner. The counsel is plain: marry right or do not marry at all. It is far better to endure the pressure of desire than to marry wrongly and live the rest of your life bearing the weight of an unhappy union.

This higher spiritual posture is also what grants certain men and women the grace to live wholly for ministry, choosing a life of celibacy—not because they failed in marriage, but because they possessed the purity that rises from above (*1 Corinthians 7:25–40, Matthew 19:10-12*).

Yet this does not gate-keep the spiritual strength needed for celibacy from those who marry. The strength to stand pure is required in both paths so that marriage may function in the beauty of holiness.

Do not be deceived—celibacy does not make a person superior or more spiritual than the believer who marries. There is no such hierarchy. In fact, marriage provides its own divine advantages, for *two are better than one*—not only for physical life, but for spiritual ascent. *(Ecclesiastes 4:9)*

As discussed, marriage and sexual intimacy within it typify Christ's relationship with the Church and the depths of true worship. Therefore, marriage becomes a divine classroom—an active looking-glass into the mysteries of God.

Celibacy is for efficiency in service, not superiority in spirituality. *(1 Corinthians 7:32-33, NLT)* Marriage remains God's perfect will for many, if not most: *"I want you to do whatever will help you serve the Lord best, with as few distractions as possible."* (*1 Corinthians 7:35, NLT*).

Entering marriage preparation—having found the one who will be your spouse and having rectified your sexual wholeness—one must reconcile personal appetites and preferences with the God-given uniqueness of their partner.

This alignment cultivates the medicine of contentment, guarding the covenant against temptation and infidelity. With maturity in Christ, we do not gaze outward; we find fulfillment in the spouse God has entrusted to us. We cultivate contentment in all circumstances because maturity empowers us to do so—for the glory of God and for the preservation of our covenant partner.

PREPARATION PRINCIPLES FOR A SOLID FOUNDATION

Healthy people make for a healthy relationship; unhealthy people make for an unhealthy one—emotionally speaking. If you carry the wrong perspective regarding the dynamics of marriage, then what you believe is right may in fact be deeply wrong (*Matthew 6:22–23*). And when the perspective is wrong, the marriage becomes unhealthy.

God does not fix marriages—He fixes people. The marriage covenant is perfect in its design; God Himself authored it. The dysfunction seen in marriages stems from the dysfunction within people. Therefore, God is in the business of restoring individuals. This is where the purity that rises from Above enters.

The upward call of God in Christ Jesus summons us into spiritual maturity—growth into Christlikeness by feeding our inner beings on the Word of God. As we have explored in depth, maturing in the Word through partnership with the Holy Spirit is the path to wholeness and freedom in God, and thus the path to wholeness for a healthy marriage.

Marriage has no problems—people do. Marriages do not break; broken people break unions. Marriage remains as intangibly perfect as it was when God created it. Yet when two spiritually mature people come together in this pure covenant, great things happen.

The glory of God shines through their union as they reflect the divine blueprint of marital function: *"Let your light shine before others, that they may see your good deeds and glorify your Father in heaven."* (*Matthew 5:16, NIV*).

To prepare for marriage, you must confront and deal with the dysfunctions in your life—emotional wounds, sexual sin, and the residual effects of past trauma.

This healing comes through maturing in Christ across the seasons that lead up to marriage. And if you are already married and struggling, this journey still applies—for both you and your spouse. The same principles of healing and purity rebuild what has been damaged.

Wrong perspectives must be corrected, because unhealthy people create unhealthy marriages. The traumas of the past must be addressed; this is the groundwork for purity in marriage.

Bad marriages do not exist—only broken individuals who carry unresolved issues. In preparing for marriage, you must bring your life into order by attaining a measure of spiritual maturity that empowers you to live in purity—sexually, emotionally, spiritually, and mentally. This is not optional; it is essential.

The more unhealthy you are, the more unhealthy your marriage will be. The more whole you are, the more wholesome your marriage will be.

While we will always carry imperfections—hence our need for Christ—marriage becomes the refining ground where we learn unconditional love, patience, consideration, and balance. It becomes the relational environment in which we better understand how God loves humanity, for marriage gives us a "type-class" of His steadfast love toward a fallen world.

Trust is what makes a marriage stand. As established, marriage is a covenant, not a contract. Thus, honesty and truth are the foundational pillars of a healthy union. To illuminate this, consider Adam and Eve—not only as historical fact (affirmed by Jesus in *Matthew 19:4–6* and *Mark 10:6–9*), but also as spiritual allegory.

The man and his wife were naked and felt no shame because they had nothing to hide. The Hebrew word for "shame," **(boosh)**, literally means to feel guilt for wrongdoing, or to feel worthless because of guilt. Their nakedness symbolized complete openness and honesty. When they sinned, they clothed themselves to hide their guilt.

It is human nature to connect what we have done with who we are. It is human nature to connect what has happened to us with our identity. This is why people carry shame for things that were never their fault.

This is why we hide behind secrets—fearing that confession will cause the other person to see us as we see ourselves. But secrecy violates the covenant. Wherever secrets live, intimacy dies. Wherever intimacy lives, secrets die.

This is why prioritizing spiritual growth in the Word is essential. The Word is truth—and truth, when allowed access, sets us free. Even during courtship, both individuals must understand the necessity of the upward call toward maturity for the sake of the health of their future marriage.

Committing to grow together in the Word with the Holy Spirit is a powerful foundation—a clarity that strengthens purity from the onset: *"Then you will know the truth, and the truth will set you free."* (John 8:32, NIV).

There is nothing you cannot be cleansed of. Truth will always liberate you. Come to terms with it through the Word of God. *"For He made Him who knew no sin to be sin for us, that we might become the righteousness of God in Him."* (2 Corinthians 5:21, NKJV).

You are no longer your past. Christ died to ensure your freedom. You are now the righteousness of God in Christ Jesus. And with this truth established in your soul, your marriage can stand in purity—and therefore in divine permanence.

Marriage is designed to change you for the better. It joins two lives so intimately and personally that it transforms the whole being. This is the secret to a great marriage: marriage is *meant* to change you, but only in a way that enhances who God created you to be. *"For we are God's workmanship, created in Christ Jesus to do good works, which God prepared in advance for us to do."* (Ephesians 2:10, NIV).

As much as we convince ourselves that all we want is our spouse's happiness, the truth is that human nature often seeks its own desires. This is why spouses may resort to subtle verbal, emotional, and mental manipulative tactics—often unknowingly—to get what they want. But this is the opposite of God's intention.

Marriage is not meant to change *who* God created you to be; it is meant to enhance *who* God created you to be. The key to a great marriage is when both partners understand their differences, appreciate each other's contributions, and seek a godly balance.

God's best for you in marriage is experienced when you release each other to become the fullness of who God intends them to be—not when you attempt to mold them into what *you* want. A great marriage flourishes when both partners have the liberty to walk in their God-given identity, encouraging and celebrating one another as they grow into the fullness of Christ's intention.

Boundaries must be established in marriage. A personal boundary is a line you set that defines what you will allow and what you will not allow—what you will tolerate and what you refuse to tolerate.

The purpose of boundaries is to protect your heart, soul, and well-being from manipulation, misuse, or abuse. In marriage—an interpersonal covenant—boundaries clearly define right from wrong behaviors.

Relationship boundaries outline acceptable and unacceptable behavior, clarifying what you are comfortable with and what you are not. These lines are not suggestions; crossing them is strictly forbidden for the sake of preserving the purity God ordained for marriage.

If you desire a healthy marriage, then *you* must become healthy—spiritually maturing into Christlikeness. Healthy people set boundaries. Unhealthy people avoid them, leaving the nuances and relational dynamics of the marriage undefined.

Undefined expectations breed confusion, hurt, misuse, and preventable emotional wounds. But when the integrity and peace of the marriage are attended to early—with maturity, clarity, and understanding—the marriage prospers.

If you want a great marriage, you must take responsibility for how you behave toward your spouse—and equally, for the behavior you permit from your spouse. Everything must be built on mutual respect, love, and understanding as God's divine design dictates.

Even the boundaries you create around one another and around your household must be rooted in the purity that comes only through the knowledge of the Word of God. This truth remains immovable: ***marriage prospers in the hands of the spiritually mature.***

A PURE MARRIAGE RELATIONSHIP: A WORTHWHILE LIFE OF PURITY

When it comes to a pure marriage—a union established upon the perfect design of God—we must understand God's principles concerning loving service, the true nature of submission, and the boundaries of what is acceptable and what violates purity in marriage.

God created marriage to make life worthwhile for both husband and wife, granting each a companion who will stand with them through the rising and falling seasons of life. It is a bond where each holds the other in purity, that the love of God may be revealed and may abound richly between them.

"Live happily with the woman you love through all the meaningless days of life that God has given you under the sun. The wife God gives you is your reward for all your earthly toil." (Ecclesiastes 9:9, NLT).

This verse establishes a foundational principle: the husband's reward in life is his wife—and the wife's reward is to be treated as one. For the husband, his wife is his treasure and his jewel, the one in whom he finds peace, home, and joy—a divine reward for life's labors.

For the wife, her reward is to be loved, cherished, prioritized, and honored. Though she may choose to work and earn, she is not required by divine command to do so; the responsibility to provide falls upon the man. She is to be cared for—not merely financially, but wholly—so that whatever work she may engage in flows from desire, not obligation.

This is the treatment worthy of a treasure. By this reality, God's principles concerning marriage place the woman more on the receiving end of loving service, while the man leads through sacrificial service. She is to be edified in the Word, continually cleansed and refreshed by the washing of Scripture.

She is to be protected and honored as the queen of the home. The husband must speak words of grace, love, encouragement, and honor over her—declaring the Word of God and standing as a priestly covering upon her life.

"Who can find a virtuous and capable wife? She is more precious than rubies. Her husband can trust her, and she will greatly enrich his life. She brings him good, not harm, all the days of her life." (Proverbs 31:10–12, NLT).

The noble woman of Proverbs 31:10–31 exemplifies this praised, mature wife. *"Her children stand and bless her. Her husband praises her: 'There are many virtuous and capable women in the world, but you surpass them all!' Charm is deceptive, and beauty does not last; but a woman who fears the LORD will be greatly praised. Reward her for all she has done. Let her deeds publicly declare her praise."* (Proverbs 31:28–31, NLT).

Both husbands and wives must therefore become mature in spirit. A mature couple understands the divine nature of true submission—a submission modeled perfectly in the life of Christ, the flawless and eternal example of a pure Husband.

PURITY IN INTIMACY

As we have established through the preparation principles for marriage, trust and faithfulness are what make a marriage stand. Wherever secrets live, intimacy dies. Wherever intimacy lives, secrets die. *In >> To >> Me >> See.* This is the principled truth of real intimacy. Thus, in the upward call of God through Christ Jesus, marital intimacy becomes a divine classroom: to gain the intimate knowledge of Christ is "to see into Him." How profound. That is intimacy—*to see into each other.* :')

Marriage is intended to join two lives together in a relationship so intimate, so personal, that it transforms their entire being. *"For we are God's workmanship, created in Christ Jesus to do good works, which God prepared in advance for us to do."* (Ephesians 2:10, NIV). Marriage is not meant to change who God created you to be; it is meant to **enhance** who God created you to be.

A great marriage is one where both partners have the liberty to be exactly who God designed them to be—encouraging one another into the fullness of that divine design. This strengthens the bond of purity in intimacy.

They learn to know each other deeply, gaining an intimate knowledge of one another. This sacred bond becomes a revelation of the purity of our covenant with Christ, giving added advantage in gaining the intimate knowledge of Him and growing in the upward call of God through Christ Jesus.

INTIMACY AND MUTUAL SUBMISSION

Marriage is an interpersonal, divine classroom—teaching us mutual submission and mutual consideration, ordering our desires to serve one another, because love "does not seek its own way." This submission is positional for the woman in marriage, established for divine order under the husband's leadership.

Yet the deeper reality calls the husband to sacrificial love, servanthood, and humility for the benefit of his wife. For him, the command is nothing less than the voluntary and wholehearted subordination of his entire life—a form of dying—following the pattern of Christ, for the betterment of his wife in every aspect of his leadership.

As believers, we are called to voluntarily place what we want under what others need, as peace-loving Christians. For the husband, this is precisely what God expects him to do for his wife in marriage. Her submission is an office—a positional grace for order. His loving service, life-subordination, and self-emptying balance the divine equation.

The principle stands: **she is his reward; hers is to be treated like one.** True love is patient, kind, gentle, and not self-seeking. It permits others their needs and desires above one's own. Therefore, it is submissive. *(1 Corinthians 13:4–5).*

PURITY IN SUBMISSION: MISCONCEPTIONS RECTIFIED

"And further, submit to one another out of reverence for Christ. For wives, this means submit to your husbands as to the Lord. For a husband is the head of his wife as Christ is the head of the church. He is the Savior of his body, the church. As the church submits to Christ, so you wives should submit to your husbands in everything. For husbands, this means love your wives, just as Christ loved the church. He gave up his life for her to make her holy and clean, washed by the cleansing of God's word. He did this to present her to himself as a glorious church without a spot or wrinkle or any other blemish. Instead, she will be holy and without fault. In the same way, husbands ought to love their wives as they love their own bodies. For a man who loves his wife actually shows love for himself. No one hates his own body but feeds and cares for it, just as Christ cares for the church. And we are members of his body. As the Scriptures say, 'A man leaves his father and mother and is joined to his wife, and the two are united into one.' This is a great mystery, but it is an

illustration of the way Christ and the church are one. So again I say, each man must love his wife as he loves himself, and the wife must respect her husband." (Ephesians 5:21–33, NLT)

Submission means "to place under." It assumes order, and it involves willingly allowing someone else to decide or choose in a matter—placing what you desire under what the other person desires. Yet many misconceptions exist about submission, especially within marriage. Therefore, it is essential to return to the biblical principles God established.

The Principle of Reciprocal Submission: Mutual Submission

Mutual submission is the foundation of all Christian relationships. God expects every believer to walk in submission toward others whenever possible. *"And further, submit to one another out of reverence for Christ."* (Ephesians 5:21, NLT).

As a mature Christian—and even more as a peace-loving spouse—you should voluntarily place what you want under what your spouse's needs. Christ Himself, the Lord of all, modeled this when He humbled Himself to wash His disciples' feet, offering loving service despite His position as Master.

He later laid down His life, ensuring that we, His bride, would receive salvation and betterment. *"For even the Son of Man came not to be served but to serve others and to give his life as a ransom for many."* (Mark 10:45, NLT).

Thus, the number one requirement for a successful marriage is mutual submission—each spouse placing their desires beneath the other's. This reciprocity births harmony, unity, and purity in the marriage covenant.

The Second Principle: Submission to God-Given Authority

God also expects believers to submit to those in positions of authority. *"Wives, submit to your own husbands, as to the Lord."* (Ephesians 5:22, NKJV). Whenever God grants responsibility, He also holds that individual accountable. *"Now, a person who is put in charge as a manager must be faithful."* (1 Corinthians 4:2, NLT).

God never assigns responsibility without also granting the authority needed to fulfill it (*Romans 13:1–4*). Therefore, because God appointed the husband as the head of the household, he carries the authority to lead—by divine design and command.

Yet a wise, Christ-honoring husband will never abuse this authority. Instead, he will cherish, protect, provide for, and honor his wife—placing her above himself. True submission is an act of love and reverence. For the wife, it becomes her crowning glory, not an oppressive burden. In a Christ-centered marriage, submission is mutual, beautiful, and life-giving—rooted not in domination or control but in humility, honor, and sacrificial love.

In this divine union, the husband is accountable to lead by servant-love, providing spiritual cleansing and encouragement by the Word. He upholds his wife spiritually, physically, and emotionally (*Ephesians 5:25*).

Marriage is a platform designed to change you; however, by God's perfect will, it must never change you in a wrong way, but rather enhance who God created you to be. It grants you the opportunity to learn in God's classroom—teaching many to further understand Him and to think and function like Him in His practical love.

Because marriage is an interpersonal relationship, we learn consideration and mutual submission, letting another's wants, needs, and desires go ahead of our own, for love does not seek its own way. In this way, both partners have freedom to express their God-given gifts without suppression.

The success of marriage depends on mutual submission and love. *"Submit to one another out of reverence for Christ."* (Ephesians 5:21, NLT). This mutual submission leaves no room for oppression; instead, it cultivates respect, honor, and joy.

Scriptural order places responsibility on husbands as leaders, balanced by their call to humility and sacrificial service, just as Christ demonstrated. Husbands speak life, grace, and affirmation over their wives, nurturing their strength rather than tearing it down. *"Husbands, love your wives and never treat them harshly."* (Colossians 3:19, NLT).

There is a submission test that determines who should submit to whose will in order to keep disorder out of the marriage dynamic. It lies in understanding what God holds each spouse responsible for. Submission is never a license for abuse or domination, but an expression of love and respect fulfilled by a mutual commitment to Christ-centered living.

Knowing what each person is responsible for determines whose desire takes precedence. God is not the author of confusion (*1 Corinthians 14:33*). This order maintains purity and shields the marriage from conflicts that lead to divorce. The test of submission is wrapped in one simple question: "Does God hold me responsible for this?"

Principle: You do not have the right to exercise authority over anything God does not hold you responsible for. This applies equally to both parties in the marriage covenant. A mature couple—understanding in-depth the biblical responsibilities of the husband and the wife (*beyond the scope of this book*)—will prosper and never fall into friction over submission.

God's design places the husband under pure and loving practice toward his wife and places the wife in the office of submission as her position in the covenant. This is true submission explained, so no one lives under misconception concerning God's inerrant principles.

It is perfectly balanced in the love of God, leaving no room for the oppression of the woman because she is commanded to submit. Instead, it elevates her as the queen of the house, for the man has the heavier call to loving-service—loving her, cherishing her, treating her like a reward, for she is his reward—and placing her wants, needs, and desires ahead of his own, following the pattern of Christ.

The woman may be called to submit, but the husband is called to "die." This dying is absolute commitment to loving service—giving his life to ensure hers is uplifted, protected, loved, cherished, and nurtured. This nurturing extends far beyond the financial, reaching into spiritual cleansing.

"For husbands, this means love your wives, just as Christ loved the church. He gave up his life for her to make her holy and clean, washed by the cleansing of God's word." (Ephesians 5:25–26, NLT). Just as Christ, the Groom of the Church, served the disciples—even washing their feet—the husband is to serve his wife (*John 13:1–17*).

A pure marriage design dictates that the husband wholly give himself in every aspect of his life for the good of his wife. This solidifies the principle of mutual submission—placing her needs, cares, well-being, and desires above his own.

His loving-service ensures she prospers into her God-ordained purpose, using his life substance as the stepping stone that lifts her higher. That is purity in marriage. Husbands are called to love their wives as Christ loved the Church, laying down His life for her.

A wise and Christ-honoring husband will never take advantage of his leadership role, for Christ never did. Though possessing all authority and Lordship—and receiving honor and submission—His humility reveals the husband's true posture: a level of loving-service so full, so sacrificial, that it rivals even the wife's submission in marriage.

This brings divine balance, leaving no room for abuse of authority, but channeling it into endless love, care, protection, and honor—only fitting for a treasure such as she is, his God-given reward.

For so long, we have viewed the equation incorrectly. When one truly understands the purity of the intimate knowledge of Christ, it becomes clear: in his leadership role, the husband bears the greater command and obligation to be the most "submissive"—in the true, purified context of sacrificial love.

Likewise, a mature and Christ-honoring wife will not undermine her husband's leadership, for doing so violates God's instruction to her. *"To live wisely and be pure, to work in their homes, to do good, and to be submissive to their husbands. Then they will not bring shame on the word of God."* (Titus 2:5, NLT).

This creates the purity of balance in marriage, and we further understand the depths of the upward call of God through Christ Jesus. The submission of the woman should therefore be sourced from a heart of love and appreciation, for it is an act of love—an acknowledgment of the sacrifices and prioritization of her that the husband, by divine design, is commanded to embody.

Her submission reciprocates the love of his life's sacrifice, just as the Church's submission to Christ reciprocates and demonstrates love and appreciation for His sacrifice. We are not oppressed in our submissive position as the Bride; rather, God blesses us for it. Thus, submission for the woman in marriage becomes her crowning glory—an expression of mutual love and mutual submission.

Let no one misunderstand the principles of God again. Marriage is perfect, and submission in marriage for the woman is her crowning, not her enslaving. Submission in marriage is a concept long misunderstood. It does not mean becoming a doormat; rather, it is an act of love—subordinating our rights to meet the needs of another first.

Christ Himself demonstrated this when He surrendered His own will to fulfill our need for salvation: *"Father, if You are willing, take this cup from Me; yet not My will, but Yours be done."* (Luke 22:42, NIV). In that single act, He subordinated His human desire beneath our eternal need, carrying out the work that secured our salvation. For One who is God, possessing all power, this humility and submission are profoundly unmatched.

How then can a husband—seeing such an example—abuse his authority over his wife, when Christ has shown the pattern of loving service, lowliness, gentleness, unconditional love, and voluntary submission? It must be a choice of love for the man, given that he may express Christ-like love.

How then can he lord over his wife after seeing this? Only through misconception and a lack of maturing into the excellent knowledge of Christ. This is wrong, and must be corrected as the Church restores the beauty of holiness to the pillar of sexuality—the purity that rises from *above.*

A benevolent father and a good husband will be the most submissive within a family once he comes to the knowledge of the Word of God and matures in it. For this is a principle: submission—especially mutual submission—is a by-product of true love (*1 Corinthians 13:4–5*). When both partners are mature in Christ—walking in the excellent knowledge of Christ—their marriage shall prosper.

In a home where both partners are strong and mature in Christ, submission is never a struggle because they understand its truth and are committed to one another's happiness.

With this understanding of the right balance for a pure marital relationship, both spouses now walk in mature understanding. And with maturity in marriage comes the greatness to prosper to the glory of God—a righteous exemplification of truth that sets a perfect example for all who observe. They will be won over by witnessing this pure and reverent adherence to God's design for marriage.

1 Peter 3:1–7 (NLT)

WIVES

"In the same way, you wives must accept the authority of your husbands. Then, even if some refuse to obey the Good News, your godly lives will speak to them without any words. They will be won over by observing your pure and reverent lives. Don't be concerned about the outward beauty of fancy

hairstyles, expensive jewelry, or beautiful clothes. You should clothe yourselves instead with the beauty that comes from within, the unfading beauty of a gentle and quiet spirit, which is so precious to God. This is how the holy women of old made themselves beautiful. They put their trust in God and accepted the authority of their husbands. For instance, Sarah obeyed her husband, Abraham, and called him her master. You are her daughters when you do what is right without fear of what your husbands might do."

HUSBANDS

"In the same way, you husbands must give honor to your wives. Treat your wife with understanding as you live together. She may be weaker than you are, but she is your equal partner in God's gift of new life. Treat her as you should so your prayers will not be hindered."

This maturity—understanding God's marital principles governing the covenant—grants purity that shields a union from divorce. It "divorce-proofs" the marriage. God hates divorce, yet He also hates domestic violence, for it breaks the covenant just as unfaithfulness does.

Both are forms of covenant-breaking, for marriage is meant to be a sanctuary of mutual love, care, tenderness, intimacy, gentleness, and support. *"The man who hates and divorces his wife," says the LORD, the God of Israel, "does violence to the one he should protect," says the LORD Almighty. "So be on your guard, and do not be unfaithful."* (Malachi 2:16, NIV)

Marriage is humanity's God-given looking-glass into His divinity. We must preserve its perfect integrity, for nothing else in this life so clearly typifies the reality of God as marriage does. Marriage is indispensable for knowing God more—deeper, richer, more tangibly. This is the depth of its purpose: to help us ascend the divine spiritual planes of maturing in Christ. Marriage becomes a launchpad into the intimate knowledge of Christ, enabling us to ascend the upward call of God—rising into the place *above*.

après moi, le déluge!

PURITY RISES FROM ABOVE

CLARION CALL

*"*A*s God's partners, we beg you not to accept this marvelous gift of God's kindness and then ignore it. For God says, 'At just the right time, I heard you. On the day of salvation, I helped you.' Indeed the 'right time' is now. Today is the day of salvation."* (2 Corinthians 6:1–2, NLT)

Having come this far in your salvation, the Upward Call of God through Christ Jesus has beckoned at you from the very first day you received salvation by believing in Christ Jesus. Purity rises from *Above*. Only through maturity in Christ—facilitated by growth through the fervent feasting upon the Word of God—can you rise to the place of strength and stature to combat the evil of the sinful nature, feeling no obligation to satisfy its lust, but walking in all the power of the Holy Spirit to put it to death along with all its misdeeds in your life.

To do this, you must be diligent and fervent—determined to mature spiritually—for as we have learned, even the health and success of your marital destiny depends upon your level of spiritual maturity. Heed the Upward Call of Maturing in Christ this day, and you shall obtain the greatness through it to carry out great exploits in this life.

You will walk the rest of your life in freedom and purity from the immorality and darkness that plagues this fallen world. You will be exempt when the floods of the enemy rise against your generation, and your standing will create the channel through which God will pour the grace to save many souls—crowning you a soul-winner for the glory of God.

If you haven't yet received the gift of salvation thus far, or if you carry the conviction for rededication after being marred by the impurities birthed from the influence of the sinful nature, then there is no harm in rededication. Align—or realign—your life to the path of righteousness.

Salvation is God's loving gift to all, and no one broken in contrition can lose it. Speaking of God:

"You were his enemies, separated from him by your evil thoughts and actions. Yet now he has reconciled you to himself through the death of Christ in his physical body. As a result, he has brought you into his own presence, and you are holy and blameless as you stand before him without a single fault. But you must continue to believe this truth and stand firmly in it. Don't drift away from the assurance you received when you heard the Good News..." (Colossians 1:21–23, NLT)

"For He has rescued us from the kingdom of darkness and transferred us into the kingdom of His dear Son, who purchased our freedom and forgave our sins." (Colossians 1:13–14, NLT)

Prayer of Surrender:

"Dear God, I know I am a sinner, and I know that my sin has separated me from You. But I believe You love me, as You declare in Your Holy Word; and because You love me, You sent Your Son Jesus to die for my sin. I believe with my heart that when Jesus died, His soul went to hell to pay the penalty for my sin. And I also believe that when all my sin was paid for, You, O God, raised Jesus from the dead, that I too may share in His resurrection and live a life of righteousness by believing in Him. Jesus, I ask that You forgive me of my sin. I put my faith in You. I believe You died for my sin, and God raised You from the dead, and I confess this with my mouth. I ask You to be the Lord of my life. Thank You for saving me. AMEN."

"Now may the God of peace make you holy in every way, and may your whole spirit and soul and body be kept blameless until our Lord Jesus Christ comes again. God will make this happen, for He who calls you is faithful." (1 Thessalonians 5:23–24, NLT)

This is what I call the Tripartite Prayer of Covering—ensuring your spirit, soul, and body is accounted for in the Upward Call for the purity that rises from *Above*. According to the Word of God, He who calls you is faithful to ensure you will make it to this desired end.

Prayer of Launching:

"Dear God, I come before you in humble submission and understanding. I pray for the attainment of spiritual maturity—for the strength for purity to stand against an immoral world that combats us with immorality. Grant me growth unhindered through the Word of God. I understand that I cannot do this without the edifying help of Your Holy Spirit, so I ask You to anoint me with Yourself. O Holy Spirit, come into my life, dear God, and help me to mature as I read the Word of God. Give me the discipline and commitment to stay true and steadfast to mature. I understand that if I don't grow the stature and muscles to fight for, and stand for purity in my spirit, and in this world for the sake of the agenda of God, then I will remain a helpless infant—taken advantage of and destroyed by the wiles of the enemy. Help me, O God. Launch me by Your Spirit into the purity that rises from 'Above!' AMEN."

And now—*"The LORD bless you and keep you; The LORD make His face shine upon you, and be gracious to you; The LORD lift up His countenance upon you, and give you peace."* (Numbers 6:24–26, NKJV)

May your spiritual growth in Christ never cease, and may you ascend to the highest of heights in the Upward Call of God through Christ Jesus—deeper into the intimate knowledge of your Lord and Savior—and forever walk in true and sustainable purity in Jesus' mighty name!

For soon the King shall stretch forth His hand and say—*"Well done, good and faithful servant... Enter into the joy of your Lord."* (Matthew 25:23, NKJV)

SHALOM and MARANATHA.

CHRIST'S Faithful Vassal,

JEHU :')

About the author

Yeshua S. Jehu, authors the five-book *Shepherd's Pouch* series. Tailored for believers, it tackles power, financial stewardship, wealth-building, destiny fulfillment, spiritual development, and sexual purity—equipping you to stand strong in integrity, mature in truth for leadership, discipleship, relationships, and personal life.

Purity Rises From Above, the *fifth installment* of the series, unveils the divine simplicity by which true purity is attained and sustained. Moving beyond the struggle and confusion that surrounds this subject, this volume reveals the singular, God-given principle that subdues the sinful nature and restores the believer to dominion through maturity in Christ. It confronts the distortions that have complicated purity and re-establishes the path in its original clarity—plain, powerful, and accessible to all who will receive it.

Through revelatory insight and anchored biblical truth, this work establishes a clear and ascending pathway into freedom—purity of mind, body, and spirit—restoring divine order to sexuality and culminating in true marital greatness in Christ Jesus. It equips the believer with right perspective, right knowledge, and spiritual precision, enabling a life where the bondage of sin is broken, strength is sustained, and purity is no longer pursued as an ideal, but lived as a reality flowing from above.

Interconnected yet standalone, each volume ensures you grow fully equipped, lacking nothing.

Connect with the Author

Follow me on social media to stay updated:
Twitter/X: @Yeshua_S_Jehu
Instagram: @Yeshua_S_Jehu

LinkedIn: @Yeshua Jehu

Stay connected—discover new updates, behind-the-scenes stories, and keep the conversation going. Connect, share, and be part of the journey.

The Shepherd's Pouch: A Five-Book Vision for Biblical Dominion

The *Shepherd's Pouch* is the visionary expression of this transformative five-book series, now brought to its divine culmination in *Purity Rises From Above*. This final installment completes the architecture—revealing that beyond formation, beyond acquisition, and even beyond preservation, there must be **purification**. For what God builds, establishes, and sustains must ultimately be rendered pure, governed, and aligned with His divine nature.

This volume unveils the crowning revelation of the series: the simplicity through which true purity is attained, the mastery over the sinful nature, and the restoration of divine order within the believer—spirit, soul, body, and even sexuality. It brings the journey to its highest expression, where freedom is not pursued as a distant hope, but established as a living reality flowing from above.

That profound progression spans the entirety of the five-book series—each work delivered with consistent excellence, interconnected as a cohesive whole, yet individually complete, satisfying, and independent. For those who desire the fullness of the Pouch, the journey is clear:

Book I opened the gate to power—revealing how to steward influence with purity, precision, and divine cunning.

Book II established the first pillar: finances and wealth—rightly ordered under God's dominion.

Book III forged identity—laying the indispensable process of transformation, growth, and becoming.

Book IV secured preservation—guarding the flame, sustaining zeal, and protecting the believer from spiritual decline.

Now, **Book V — *Purity Rises From Above*** completes it all—bringing the believer into mastery, where the sinful nature is subdued, divine order is restored, and life is governed from a place of purity that descends from above.

For those who would carry the *Shepherd's Pouch* in its fullness, each installment stands ready—forming, building, preserving, and now perfecting the vessel unto the glory of God.

There are the three pillars of human society from which dominion over the earth becomes possible through God's divinely set principles—pillars upon which this entire series teaches passionately: **Sexuality, Religion/Spirituality,** and **Finances/Wealth.**

These are the roots of dominion, power, and influence, without which the church cannot wield transformative power for divine effect. Discover how these pillars are rooted in Scripture, first revealed in Genesis 1:28 as the eternal formula for power, as you journey through the entirety of this series.

Experience the *"fruitfulness"* of true spiritual life that pleases God and re-shapes society; the divine *"multiplication"* born from the purity of sexuality, radiating righteous integrity across every avenue of life; the knowledge to build wealth that empowers you to *"subdue"* the earth and enact physical change with authority; and finally, the *"dominion"* that manifests as you master these three pillars through the wisdom and revelation of the Holy Spirit—applied with unshakable practicality.

"Then God blessed them, and God said to them, 'Be fruitful and multiply; fill the earth and subdue it; have dominion over the fish of the sea, over the birds of the air, and over every living thing that moves on the earth.'" (Genesis 1:28, NKJV)

Unlock the complete series and step into your divine authority. God bless you!

Also by Yeshua S. Jehu

THE SHEPHERD'S POUCH Series

Book 1: The 48 Laws of Power Biblically

Book 2: Money Biblically

Book 3: The Principle of Becoming

Book 4: The Five Guardians of Spiritual Fervour

Book 5: Purity Rises from Above

"Dare to complete the pouch? Interlock power, influence, purity, and spiritual vitality—unlock their divine interconnectivity. *Hope to see you in the next volume, fully armed."* :')